IMAGES
of America

CINCINNATI'S
UNDERGROUND RAILROAD

IMAGES
of America

CINCINNATI'S
UNDERGROUND RAILROAD

Richard Cooper and Dr. Eric R. Jackson

ARCADIA
PUBLISHING

Published by Arcadia Publishing
Charleston, South Carolina

Printed in the United States of America

Library of Congress Control Number: 2013947908

For all general information, please contact Arcadia Publishing:
Telephone 843-853-2070
Fax 843-853-0044
E-mail sales@arcadiapublishing.com
For customer service and orders:
Toll-Free 1-888-313-2665

Visit us on the Internet at www.arcadiapublishing.com

This volume is dedicated to the memories of all those individuals who sought to escape bondage throughout the history of the United States as well as those who continue to work for freedom and equality everywhere today.

CONTENTS

ACKNOWLEDGMENTS

We could not have completed this project without the encouragement, support, and assistance of numerous individuals. We are greatly indebted and give much thanks to our editors Jill Nunn and Mary Margaret Schley. Their patience, understanding, and vision greatly inspired us to continue in the process despite the hardships that were encountered in the acquisition of various items. There is no question that without Jill and Mary Margaret, this book would not have been published with such precision and care.

There are many other people and institutions we also wish to thank for their valuable contributions to the research and completion of this book. We always will be thankful for Linda Bailey, Claire Smittle, and Anne Shepard at the Cincinnati Historical Society-Library as well as Jamie Glavic and Lily Birkhimer at the Ohio Historical Society. Many of the photographs and other resources obtained from these facilities played a very critical role in the development and completion of this volume. We also would like to thank various staff members of the Cincinnati–Hamilton County Public Library as well as Mike Miller at the Carolina Digital Library and Archives. Special thanks also must go to Northern Kentucky University, particularly Drs. Bill Landon, Brian Hackett, and Paul Tenkotte for their professional support and guidance as this project was developed.

The preparation and writing time needed to complete this book was far beyond what we had anticipated. Thus, we will be forever thankful to a number of people for welcoming us into their offices and institutions to discuss this project hundreds of times, such as Dina Bailey, Cori Sisler, and Carl Westmoreland of the National Underground Railroad Freedom Center, as well as the financial support of the US Department of Education. We will be forever in your debt.

It is impossible to thank all the individuals whose personal strength, everlasting support, and unlimited patience helped us produce this book. However, the most important people are Eric's wife, B.J. Jackson, and Rich's parents, Marie and Richard Cooper. Much love and thanks goes to you all.

INTRODUCTION

The waters of the Ohio River provided a real and complex barrier for the young nation for nearly a century after the American Revolution ended. On one hand, this waterway symbolized, in general, freedom for thousands of enslaved African Americans who had absconded from their horrible life as a worker on a plantation. On the other hand, the Ohio River was used to transport thousands of enslaved persons of color down the river to the deep South and into a life that was dominated by the Cotton Belt market. In essence, the Ohio River (or as some people called it, the River Jordan) signified both freedom and slavery simultaneously. The paradox that played out along the Ohio also helped to foster a number of cities and towns that became linked to the origin, development, and legacy of the Underground Railroad. One such city was Cincinnati, known by some as "Porkopolis" or the "Queen City." During the antebellum period, because of its location on the Ohio River, as well as the growth of a strong local African American community, the city became a major destination for thousands of individuals who sought to gain their freedom through the use of the Underground Railroad.

This book seeks to document and illustrate this story from a variety of perspectives by examining specific individuals, neighborhoods, organizations, and businesses. For example, on a peaceful evening in 1842, John P. Parker quietly boarded a ship that was docked in the harbor of New Orleans. Scared but determined, Parker knew that his days as an enslaved African American were numbered. Several hours later, the vessel set sail up the Mississippi River with Parker safely hidden on board. Along the way, young John admired the scenery as if he was a passenger on an ocean cruise. This latest attempt to gain his freedom brought Parker to New Albany, Indiana, Cincinnati, and eventually Ripley, Ohio. Once in Ripley, Parker, along with Rev. John Rankin, began to assist thousands of other black Americans on their journey to freedom.

Several years earlier, in 1838, Frederick Douglass (formerly known as Frederick Augustus Washington Bailey) took flight from his Baltimore, Maryland, plantation. After much planning, young Douglass began his journey to freedom when he acquired a set of "free papers" from an African American sailor he had known for several months. Using forged free papers, Douglass eventually was able to board a train headed to Philadelphia. As the train began to move down the tracks, a sense of excitement fell upon him. However, this feeling quickly disappeared when he became involved in an unexpected conversation with a free African American passenger. Douglass began to think that his time as a fugitive was about to end. However, after a close call with the approaching ticket-taker that could have revealed his identity, Douglass safely continued north to Philadelphia, New York City, and eventually Boston.

About a decade later, Ellen and William Craft devised a secret but dangerous plan to escape from enslavement in Georgia. On a bright morning, Ellen awoke and began to dress in clothes that made her look like a white slave owner. Several minutes later, William, her husband, appeared as Ellen's African American slave. The two of them quickly packed some items and left their plantation. Although neither Ellen nor William could not read or write, their plan worked almost perfectly.

Several months later, in September 1844, Lewis Hayden and his family escaped from slavery in Lexington, Kentucky. However, Delia Webster and Calvin Fairbanks, the young white couple who aided them, in some ways came to be far better known then Hayden. During a five year period, Webster and Fairbanks helped hundreds of African Americans escape bondage throughout the Bluegrass state. However, their fame worked against them when the two were arrested in 1844 on their way to Lexington to help free more enslaved African Americans. Webster was sentenced to two years in prison, while Fairbanks was sentenced to five to fifteen years in the state penitentiary. He severed his time until Kentucky governor John Crittendon pardoned him on August 28, 1849.

The journeys, comments, and activities of Parker, Douglass, the Crafts, Delia Webster, Calvin Fairbanks, and thousands of others illustrate that the path to freedom was hard, complex, long, mysterious, terrifying, and dangerous, but it was still worth the sacrifice for those who were willing to try anything to obtain freedom. This quest became more difficult with the end of the American Revolution, the ratification of the US Constitution, and the implementation of the Fugitive Slave Acts of 1793 and 1850. Despite these laws and decrees, thousands of people, African Americans and Caucasians, rich and poor, Christians and non-Christians, came together to help black American fugitives gain their freedom. Thanks to Congressional actions and National Park Service initiatives of the 1990s, as well as the opening of the National Underground Railroad Freedom Center in 2004, this history remains alive in the minds of many Americans.

The most popular vision of the Underground Railroad, however, is of a handful of fugitive African Americans being assisted in their escape by one or more well-meaning and progressive whites, particularly Quakers. Indeed, such episodes did occur quite often. However, an abundance of historical evidence does exist showing that thousands of free African Americans assisted their black American brothers and sisters escape enslavement and gain freedom. Our book on Cincinnati's Underground Railroad will demonstrate how the history and legacy of this powerful subject, which many scholars have called the first multicultural, multi-class, human rights movement in the history of the United States, and perhaps the world, can help to inspire a cadre of freedom fighters and social justice trailblazers today.

The history and legacy of the Underground Railroad and the history and legacy of Cincinnati are a natural fit. This region symbolized the contradictions, struggle, and perseverance of a select group of people, from various classes, cultures, ethnicities, and races, who formed a seemingly unbreakable relationship, as well as a front line of freedom and equality that would define a nation for centuries.

One

Slavery and Abolition

Declaration of Independence. Written in 1776 by Thomas Jefferson, this document helped to ignite the War of Independence. It would later have great importance to persons of African descent with the phrase "all men are created equal," guaranteeing the rights to life, liberty, and the pursuit of happiness. (Courtesy of the Library of Congress.)

THOMAS JEFFERSON. Born in 1743 in Shadwell, Virginia, Thomas Jefferson lived abroad as the young nation's diplomat to France. During the Constitutional Convention, he initially did not support the US Constitution, but changed his mind after the Bill of Rights was added. During his presidency, Jefferson bought the Louisiana Purchase from France in 1803, which doubled the size of the country, and initiated the official Indian removal policies of the young nation. After retiring from the presidency in 1808, Jefferson returned to Monticello, led a campaign to build the University of Virginia, and subsequently served as the institution's first president. Throughout his lifetime, Jefferson also owned over 600 persons of color. While he wrote of his deep moral anguish about slavery, he was perpetually in debt and thus never freed more than a handful of his own slaves. Recently, several scholars have uncovered evidence that Jefferson had a relationship with one of his enslaved African American woman, Sally Hemmings, and fathered at least one of her children. (Courtesy of the Library of Congress.)

THE CONSTITUTION. In 1787, delegates from 12 states met in Philadelphia and created the US Constitution. On the topic of human bondage, the Constitution allowed for the Atlantic slave trade to continue until 1808 and made it possible for states to count enslaved African Americans as three-fifths of a person for the purpose of determining a state's representation in the House of Representatives. (Courtesy of the Library of Congress.)

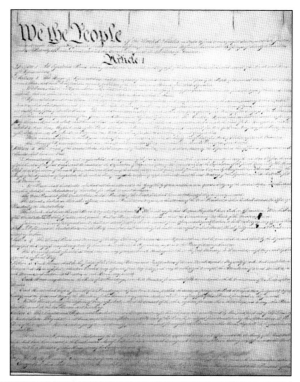

FUGITIVE SLAVE LAW OF 1793. During the Constitutional Convention of 1787, a group of proslavery men demanded that measures be enacted to stop rebellions and runaways. As a result, the foundation of the Fugitive Slave Act of 1793 was written, which provided that persons "held to service or labour in one State, escaping into another . . . shall be delivered up on claim of the party to whom such service or labour may be due." (Courtesy of the Library of Congress.)

BENJAMIN FRANKLIN. Born in 1706 in Boston, the young Franklin was not a vocal supporter of human bondage, but he did own two enslaved African Americans. However, with the end of the American Revolution, Franklin became a staunch antislavery activist who eventually freed his enslaved persons of color and also championed the education of African Americans in numerous articles and essays. (Courtesy of the Library of Congress.)

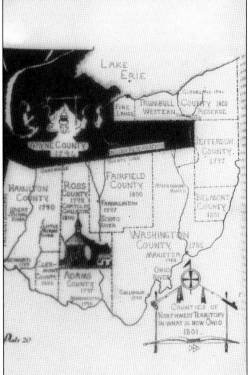

THE NORTHWEST ORDINANCE. The most important achievement of the Articles of Confederation was the plan of Congress to develop the lands west of the Appalachian Mountains. Based on many of Thomas Jefferson's governmental ideas, Congress created and adopted the Northwest Ordinance of 1787, which outlawed slavery in the new western territories and also specified that the sale of some lands would provide for support of schools. (Courtesy of the Public Library of Cincinnati and Hamilton County.)

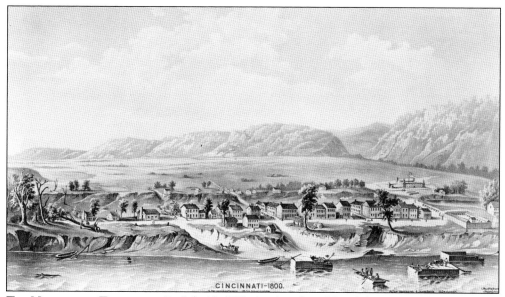

CINCINNATI-1800.

THE NORTHWEST TERRITORY. On July 13, 1787, the Articles of Confederation enabled Congress to pass the Northwest Ordinance, which led to the creation of the Northwest Territory. Settlers had started to move into the region that would become the city of Cincinnati as early as 1788, but the city was not incorporated as a village until 1802 and was not an official city until 1819. (Courtesy of the Cincinnati Historical Society.)

WHIPPING SCARS OF RUNAWAY SLAVE GORDON. Individuals who used enslaved African Americans as laborers on plantations, small farms, and in their homes frequently offered incentives to induce their captives to perform well. Some of the most popular incentives were days off work or additional food and clothing. However, enslavement, by definition, is forced labor based on the threat of physical punishment or controlled violence. This image shows the scars that resulted from repeated whippings, illustrating that violence was inherent in the system of human bondage. (Courtesy of the National Underground Railroad Freedom Center.)

HARPERS WEEKLY SLAVE AUCTION, ABUSE OF SLAVERY. In the Americas, slave auctions were used until the end of the Atlantic slave trade. By 1860, the average field hand could be purchased for nearly $40,000 in today's money. Enslaved people who were sold in southern slave ports quite possibly could have traveled down the Ohio River, past the city of Cincinnati. The image here depicts a group of enslaved individuals being viewed before an auction. (Courtesy of the National Underground Railroad Freedom Center.)

RECEIPT FOR PURCHASE OF AN ENSLAVED PERSON. The profits gained from owning an enslaved person were enormous. Indeed, some enslaved African Americans could be worth almost $1,000. However, there were some shortcomings within this "peculiar institution," such as the fact that most whites (and the law) viewed enslaved black Americans as property, which meant taxes had to be paid. Pictured here is a receipt of purchase that an owner could use when paying their taxes on their human property. (Courtesy of the National Underground Railroad Freedom Center.)

COURT DOCUMENT APPROVING THE SALE OF A YOUNG ENSLAVED CHILD. Throughout the antebellum period, as owners trimmed the number of excess enslaved persons that they owned from their workforces or switched their labor system from slave labor to wage labor, they sold men, women, and children to nearby slave traders. This document represents one example of a child involved in this economic machine. (Courtesy of the National Underground Railroad Freedom Center.)

RICHARD ALLEN. Born an enslaved person in 1760 in Philadelphia, Richard Allen converted to Methodism as a young man and eventually helped to form the African Society of Philadelphia in 1787 and subsequently a separate Methodist church for African Americans in 1794, also in the "City of Brotherly Love." Many of these facilities were used to harbor escaped African Americans during the years of the Underground Railroad. (Courtesy of the Library of Congress.)

15

BETHEL AME CHURCH. Mother Bethel African Methodist Episcopal (AME) Church was the first African Methodist Episcopal church in the nation, founded in Philadelphia in 1794 by Richard Allen. Allen founded Mother Bethel AME after the church he had been attending, St. George's Methodist Episcopal Church in Philadelphia, began to segregate its parishioners by race for an unknown reason. (Courtesy of the Library of Congress.)

WALKER'S

A P P E A L,

IN FOUR ARTICLES,

TOGETHER WITH

A PREAMBLE,

TO THE

COLORED CITIZENS OF THE WORLD,

BUT IN PARTICULAR, AND VERY EXPRESSLY TO THOSE OF THE

UNITED STATES OF AMERICA.

Written in Boston, in the State of Massachusetts, Sept. 28, 1829.

SECOND EDITION, WITH CORRECTIONS, &c.

BY DAVID WALKER.

1830.

DAVID WALKER'S APPEAL. During the early antebellum period, the assault on the system of human bondage in the United States began to shift to a more militant perspective that did not accept either colonization or gradualism as key components to end the peculiar institution. One individual who represented this new era was David Walker, who advocated the use of violence to overturn the system in his pamphlet *Appeal . . . to the Colored Citizens of the World.* (Courtesy of the Library of Congress.)

NAT TURNER'S REBELLION. Born in 1800 on the Virginia plantation of Benjamin Turner in Southampton, Nat Turner was allowed to learn how to read, write, and study the Bible at a young age. Believing that God had told him to start the rebellion, in 1831 Turner and six other enslaved African Americans managed to secure some arms and horses and eventually enlisted some 75 others to begin the insurrection that resulted in the murder of 51 whites. (Courtesy of the Library of Congress.)

WILLIAM LLOYD GARRISON. Born in Newburyport, Massachusetts, in 1805, William Lloyd Garrison eventually became one of the nation's most important and fiery abolitionists. In 1831, Garrison published the first edition of his own antislavery newspaper, the *Liberator*, which continued his untamed assault on the system of enslavement despite constant personal threats and harassment from proslavery individuals and groups. (Courtesy of the Library of Congress.)

THE LIBERATOR. *The Liberator* was a weekly newspaper primarily published by abolitionist William Lloyd Garrison from January 1, 1831, to December 29, 1865. This paper was the most influential antislavery periodical during the antebellum period. Published in Boston, the *Liberator* claimed that it had a paid circulation of only 3,000 subscribers. However, it reached a much wider audience with its uncompromising and fiery advocacy for the immediate end to the institution of enslavement. In the North, Garrison's message of moral suasion challenged moderate reformers to apply the principles of the Declaration of Independence to all people, regardless of color. Fearful slave owners in the South believed that *The Liberator* represented the majority opinion of northerners, causing hundreds of southerners to react militantly by defending slavery as a "positive good" and by passing even more legislation aimed at repressing all possible opposition to its peculiar institution. In the end, Garrison's publication further altered the course of the American antislavery movement by insisting that abolition, rather than African colonization, was the answer to the problem of slavery. (Courtesy of the Library of Congress.)

ANTISLAVERY SOCIETIES. Before the articulation of the concept of Manifest Destiny, the American Antislavery Society (AASS) was created and quickly became the most significant abolitionist organization of the 1830s. Primarily based on the views of William Lloyd Garrison, who in 1831 called for the creation of an antislavery movement that was dedicated to the immediate, uncompensated emancipation and equal rights of African Americans throughout the United States, a national antislavery convention was held in Philadelphia in December 1833. At the event, a biracial group was organized that called itself the American Antislavery Society, whose members pledged their allegiance to the immediate destruction of the system of human bondage. Several residents of Ohio attended the convention, including Theodore Weld, Arthur Tappan (right), and Lewis Tappan (below). These same men helped to establish the Ohio Anti-Slavery Society in 1835. (Both, courtesy of the Library of Congress.)

HARRIET TUBMAN. Born into enslavement in Bucktown, Maryland, in 1820, as a young child Tubman was hit in the head while trying to protect another enslaved African American and suffered an injury that led her to have sudden blackouts throughout her life. Nevertheless, on her first attempt to escape, she trekked through hundreds of unknown woods at night, found shelter, and was aided by several free African Americans and Quakers until she reached freedom in Philadelphia with William Still's Vigilance Committee. After hearing that her niece and her children would soon be sold, she arranged to meet them in Baltimore and usher them north to freedom. It was the first of numerous trips Tubman made to the South as she led almost 300 enslaved African Americans to freedom. During the Civil War, Tubman served as a spy, scout, and nurse for the Union Army. When the government refused to give her a pension for her wartime service, she sold vegetables and fruit door-to-door and lived on the proceeds from her biography. (Courtesy of the Ohio Historical Society.)

FREDERICK DOUGLASS. Born into enslavement in 1817 near Tuckahoe, Maryland, Frederick Augustus Washington Baily was taught how to read as a house servant, but at the age of 16 he became a field-hand. In 1838, he escaped and settled in New Bedford, Massachusetts, where he took the name Frederick Douglass. After his initial speech before the Massachusetts Anti-Slavery Society in 1841, Douglass became a regular speaker for the abolition movement. (Courtesy of the Library of Congress.)

COMPROMISE OF 1850. Sen. Henry Clay (pictured) crafted the Compromise of 1850, which proposed the admission of California into the Union as a free state and the elimination of the slave trade (but not the institution of enslavement itself) in Washington, DC, and offered the creation of a strong fugitive slave law to make it easier for owners to recapture their runaways. Also, the states of Utah and New Mexico would be organized without any mention of enslavement. (Courtesy of the Library of Congress.)

FUGITIVE SLAVE ACT OF 1850. With the adoption of the Compromise of 1850, the Fugitive Slave Act of 1850 took effect, which created bitter resentment and division between African American and white abolitionists and made the institution of enslavement an emotional and personal issue for many white Americans. The new law directed federal marshals to aid private citizens (such as slaveholders) in pursuing and returning fugitives. (Courtesy of the Library of Congress.)

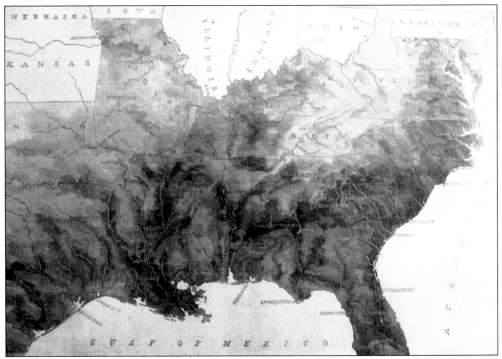

HARPERS WEEKLY SLAVE POPULATION. By 1860, the total United States population was more than 31 million people. This number included nearly four million enslaved people living in the South. In both South Carolina and Mississippi, the slave populations made up over 50 percent of the total population. (Courtesy of the National Underground Railroad Freedom Center.)

Two

RIVER OF SLAVERY, RIVER OF FREEDOM

THE CITY OF CINCINNATI. Being located on the Ohio River in Cincinnati, the sixth largest city in the nation during the 1850s, presented a wealth of economic opportunities for those who wanted to take advantage of the emerging pork packing and steamboat industries. Simultaneously, the Queen City became a safe haven for thousands of fugitive African Americans who sought to gain their freedom. (Courtesy of the Cincinnati Historical Society.)

CINCINNATI AND THE OHIO RIVER. While African Americans who lived north of the Ohio River were free, they still faced harassment and persecution from Cincinnati's pro-slavery majority. The rights of African American Cincinnatians were minimal at best and their very safety was precarious, with gangs on the lookout to kidnap and sell them into slavery. The city's emerging steamboat industry granted employment opportunities for African Americans and provided a way to transport black Americans escaping from the South to the North without detection. (Courtesy of the Cincinnati Historical Society.)

CINCINNATI'S CONNECTION TO THE INTERNAL SLAVE TRADE. The internal or domestic slave trade illustrated the falseness of the slaveholding-class claim that enslavement was a benign institution. Driven primarily by economic necessity, large profits, or a desire to curtail the notion of running away, owners in the upper South, as well as in lands that bordered parts of the Ohio Valley region, developed complex plans to expand the institution. (Courtesy of the Cincinnati Historical Society.)

OHIO ANTI-SLAVERY SOCIETY. In 1832, the New England Anti-Slavery Society was formed; within five years, it had several hundred local chapters, primarily in Massachusetts, New York, and Ohio. In late 1833, William Lloyd Garrison allied with black and white abolitionists to form the American Anti-Slavery Society (AASS) which had, as associate members, interracial female antislavery societies in Philadelphia and Boston. This society also grew quickly and had almost a quarter of a million members by 1838. In Cincinnati, Garrison helped to lead the antislavery crusade. His publications were so powerful and potent that a reward for his capture was issued by a group of white citizens. (Courtesy of the Cincinnati Historical Society.)

30 Dollars Reward.

RAN away from the fubfcriber, living at a Poft Office at White Plains, White county, ftate of Tenneffee, on the main road leading from Nafhville to Knoxville, on the night of the 4th inft. a Negro man, named

MOSES,

between 35 and 40 years of age, about 5 feet 8 or 9 inches high, well fet, broad fhouldered, bow-thigh'd, the whites of his eyes are re-markably red, a fmall piece off one of his thumbs, though the nail is ftill on and very long. He took with him fundry cloathing, to wit : a new pair of leather overalls, neatly made with a watch pocket, and a white pair of cotton ones, a brown hunting fhirt, with a cape on it, a grey coating under jacket, and other cloathing not remembered at prefent. Alfo a rifle gun, bucfkin fhot bag, with two or three rows of fringes round it, and took with him a bay Horse, about five feet high, a ftar in his forehead, fhod all round, branded on the rump with a ftirrup iron ; a little black dog very much like a cub bear, ears and tail cut off. I followed him as far as Lexington, (Ky.) and then underftood he certainly would crofs the Ohio and go on to Urbana, on Mad-river, in the ftate of Ohio.

I will pay the above reward, together with all reafonable expences, to any perfon who will take up faid Negro and confine him in any jail in the fttate of Ohio, or in Wafhing-ton or Lexington jails, Kentucky, and write me fhortly fo that I can get him again.——— Or I will pay ONE HUNDRED DOL-LARS to any perfon who will deliver him at my houfe.

N. B. He is handy with Carpenters tools.

DANIEL ALEXANDER,
Poft Mafter, White Plains.
December 15, 1809.   66 6t

NOTICE.

RUNAWAY SLAVE AD. As a result of increased numbers of runaway enslaved individuals who escaped during the antebellum period, owners began to produce hundreds of advertisements throughout the Ohio Valley region, especially in Cincinnati. Seeking the return of their property, owners wrote out tens of thousands of notices that included descriptions of special or unique facial features, speech patterns, intellectual qualities, skin color, gender, and other features that might lead to the recapture of their slave. (Courtesy of the Cincinnati Historical Society.)

JOHN MALVIN. Not all African Americans who traveled to Canada to live were former enslaved persons looking to escape the 1850 Fugitive Slave Act. Some free black Americans moved to Canada to avoid the continuous racism and racial prejudice of the United States throughout the antebellum period. One such person was John Malvin, a former resident of Cincinnati who had originally moved to the Queen City during the 1820s. (Courtesy of the Ohio Historical Society.)

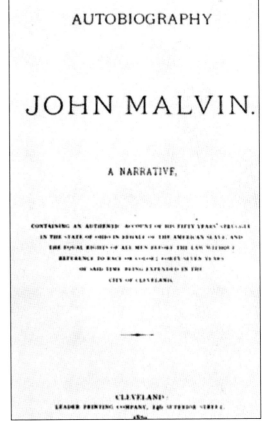

AUTOBIOGRAPHY

JOHN MALVIN.

A NARRATIVE,

CONTAINING AN AUTHENTIC ACCOUNT OF HIS FIFTY YEARS' STRUGGLE IN THE STATE OF OHIO IN BEHALF OF THE AMERICAN SLAVE, AND THE EQUAL RIGHTS OF ALL MEN BEFORE THE LAW WITHOUT REFERENCE TO RACE OR COLOR; FORTY-SEVEN YEARS OF SAID TIME BEING EXPENDED IN THE CITY OF CLEVELAND.

CLEVELAND:
LEADER PRINTING COMPANY, 146 SUPERIOR STREET.
1879.

JOHN RANKIN. Born on February 4, 1793, in Tennessee, John Rankin attended Washington College in Virginia, became a minister in the Presbyterian Church, and quickly dedicated himself to the destruction of the system of enslavement throughout the nation. In 1818, Revered Rankin formed an antislavery society in Carlisle, Kentucky, but eventually fled the state and moved to Ripley, Ohio, where enslavement was illegal. While many Ohioans opposed the ending of the peculiar institution, the Buckeye state generally was more receptive to abolitionists. Once in Ripley, Reverend Rankin and several of his sons began to participate in various Underground Railroad activities. The Rankin home stood on a 300-foot-high hill that overlooked the Ohio River, where he and his sons would signal runaways in Kentucky with lanterns when it was safe for them to cross the river. Harriet Beecher Stowe immortalized Rankin's efforts to help African Americans in her book *Uncle Tom's Cabin*, with the Rankin home being the first stop in Ohio for Eliza, one of the book's main characters, as she sought freedom in the North. (Courtesy of the Cincinnati Historical Society.)

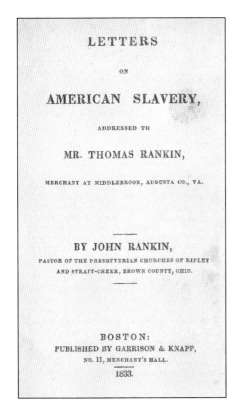

JOHN RANKIN'S *LETTERS ON AMERICAN SLAVERY*. During his first few years in Ripley, Ohio, Reverend Rankin learned that his brother Thomas, a merchant in Augusta County, Virginia, had purchased several enslaved persons of color; Rankin became so outraged that he began to write a series of antislavery letters to his brother that were published by an editor of the local Ripley newspaper, the *Castigator*, and subsequently became a book titled *Letters on American Slavery*. (Both, courtesy of the Cincinnati Historical Society.)

LETTERS ON SLAVERY.

LETTER I.

My Dear Brother,

I received yours of the 2d December, with mingled sensations of pleasure and pain ; it gave me pleasure to hear of your health, and pain to hear of your purchasing slaves. I consider involuntary slavery, a never failing fountain of the grossest immorality, and one of the deepest sources of human misery ; it hangs like the mantle of night over our republic, and shrouds its rising glories. I sincerely pity the man who tinges his hand in the unhallowed thing that is fraught with the tears, and sweat, and groans, and blood of hapless millions of innocent, unoffending people.

A mistaken brother, who has manifested to me a kind and generous heart, claims my strongest sympathies. When I see him involved in what is both sinful and dangerous, shall I not strive to liberate him? Does he wander from the paths of rectitude, and shall not fraternal affection pursue, and call him from the verge of ruin, and the unperceived precipice of wo, to

LANE THEOLOGICAL SEMINARY. In 1829, Lane Seminary was built in Cincinnati. It was named after brothers Ebenezer and William Lane, who pledged $4,000 for the construction of the school, which produced numerous well-known abolitionists such as Theodore Weld and John G. Fee. One of the first books that the students read was Reverend Rankin's *Letters on American Slavery.* (Courtesy of the Cincinnati Historical Society.)

LANE DEBATES. During the early 1800s, many Protestant seminaries were interested in sending pastors westward to the new territories. Because Ohio was a free state, many Presbyterian and Congregationalist settlers came here, specifically to Cincinnati. Lane Seminary became the site of a series of famous debates on the topic of enslavement. (Courtesy of the Cincinnati Historical Society.)

REV. JOHN G. FEE. Born in Bracken County, Kentucky, in 1816, John G. Fee was raised in a slaveholding family. After college he finished his undergraduate career at Miami University, in Oxford, Ohio, and enrolled into Cincinnati's Lane Seminary, where the heated debates over the issues of slavery and abolition had a profound effect on him. Because of his radical antislavery opinions, Fee's father eventually disowned him. (Courtesy of the Ohio Historical Society.)

JAMES BRADLEY. At the age of three, young James Bradley was stolen from his African family and brought to South Carolina, where he was almost immediately sold to a slaveholder from Pendleton County, Kentucky. Several years later, Bradley's owner decided to move his family to Arkansas, and soon James developed a plan to purchase his freedom. Once free, he attended Lane Seminary and eventually became the first African American student at Oberlin College. (Courtesy of Richard Cooper.)

THEODORE DWIGHT WELD.
Born on November, 23, 1803,
in Hampton, Connecticut,
Theodore Dwight Weld
eventually became a prominent
reformer, educator, and
abolitionist. In 1819, he
enrolled into the Phillips
Andover Academy, but had
to withdraw due to various
health problems. However, by
1833, with his health problems
behind him, Weld became a
student again and eventually a
professor at the Lane Seminary
in Cincinnati. (Courtesy of
the Ohio Historical Society.)

**A LETTER BY JOHN RANKIN
ABOUT LANE SEMINARY.** This is
the cover page to a 31-page essay
titled "Review of the Statement of
the Faculty of Lane Seminary in
Relation to the Recent Difficulties
in that Institution," which was
written by Rev. John Rankin
of Ripley, Ohio. In the essay,
Reverend Rankin, pastor of the
Presbyterian Church of Ripley,
defends students who in 1834
established an antislavery society
at Lane Seminary. (Courtesy of
the Ohio Historical Society.)

31

JAMES BIRNEY. Born in 1792 in Danville, Kentucky, as the son of a wealthy slave owning family, Birney was educated at Princeton and eventually became a successful lawyer. However, he gave up his career as state senator in Kentucky and then Alabama to work to end the system of human bondage. In 1832, he became a member of the American Colonization Society. He founded the abolitionist newspaper *The Philanthropist* in 1836 in Cincinnati. (Courtesy of the Ohio Historical Society.)

ABOLITIONISTS BEWARE. When Birney restarted the publication of *The Philanthropist,* a mob of local whites went on a rampage throughout the city, intent on destroying Birney's press for good as well as harassing members of the free African American community. A local proslavery group began to post advertisements that warned abolitionists of the treatment they might receive if they entered the state of Ohio. (Courtesy of the Cincinnati Historical Society.)

ABOLITIONISTS
BEWARE.

THE Citizens of Cincinnati, embracing every class, interested in the prosperity of the City, sat-ed that the business of the place is receiving .... stab from the wicked and misguided oper tions of the abolitionists, are resolved to arrest their course. The destruction of their Press on the night of the 12th Instant, may be taken as a warning. As there are some worthy citizens engaged in the unholy cause of annoying our southern neighbors, they are appealed to, to pause before they bring things to a crisis. If an attempt is made to re-establish their press, it will be viewed as an act of defiance to an already outraged community, and on their heads be the result which will follow.

Every kind of expostulation and remonstrance has been resorted to in vain---longer patience would be criminal. The plan is matured to eradicate an evil which every citizen feels is undermining his business and property.

Stuck up on the corner of the Streets just before the mob, July 1836

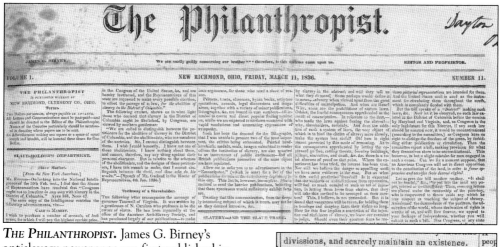

THE PHILANTHROPIST. James G. Birney's antislavery newspaper was first published in Mount Pleasant, Ohio, in September 1817. Its first editor was Charles Osborn, who was a member of the Society of Friends. Osborn called for an immediate end to slavery and hoped his paper would educate white northerners about the injustice of the system of enslavement. *The Philanthropist* was the first antislavery newspaper in the United States. Osborn emerged as one of the leading abolitionists in Ohio because of the paper. Other prominent abolitionists joined *The Philanthropist's* writing stable, including Benjamin Lundy, who contributed several articles. In October 1818, Elisha Bates acquired the newspaper from Osborn and continued to publish it until 1822. Several years later, in 1838, James Birney published another antislavery newspaper, also titled *The Philanthropist*. (Both, courtesy of the Cincinnati Historical Society.)

divisions, and scarcely maintain an existence.

S. M.

Increase of Dirty Work.

"We hold these truths to be self evident—that all men are created equal; that they are endowed by their Creator with certain unalienable rights; that, among these, are life, *liberty*, and the pursuit of happiness."—*Dec. of Independence.*

WE DECLARE—that all men are born equally free and have certain, natural, inherent, and unalienable rights—amongst which are the enjoying, and defending life and LIBERTY, acquiring, possessing and protecting property, and pursuing and obtaining happiness and safety."—*Constitution of Ohio.*

"There shall be neither slavery nor involuntary servitude in this state, otherwise than for the punishment of crimes, whereof the party shall have been duly convicted."—*Constitution of Ohio.*

Now, to all, who have no manner of respect for the above propositions—to all the genuine DOUGH-FACES of the land, the following proclamation is addressed.

[*From the Cincinnati Whig.*]

$100 REWARD.

Ranaway from the subscriber, in Washington county, Va., on Saturday night, the 28th May, a negro boy by the name of ADAM, (or he calls himself Watson) about 30 years old, black complexion, about 5 feet 10 or 11 inches high, thick lips, quick spoken, rather a coarse voice, short face and low forehead, and weighing about 170. He had on when he left a blue broad-cloth suit of clothes. It is probable that he is in possession of free-papers, and will change his name. He can read print.

The above reward will be given if he is apprehended out of the state, and secured in any jail so that I get him again, or $25 if he is apprehended in this state. It is unknown where he will aim to go.

ROBERT MEEK.

June 1, 1836.

The Charleston (Kenawha,) Banner, Maysville (Ky.) Eagle, and Cincinnati (Ohio) Whig, will please insert the above 4 times, and forward their accounts to this office for payment.—*Virginia Statesmen.*

ANTI-SLAVERY ECCLESIASTICS.

The Protestant Methodist Conference of Vermont, at their last annual meeting passed the following

33

DESTROYING JAMES G. BIRNEY'S PRESS. In 1836, James Birney began to publish another antislavery newspaper titled *The Philanthropist* in Cincinnati. Birney advocated an immediate end to slavery and also believed that African Americans were entitled to equal rights and opportunities. Many white Cincinnatians opposed Birney's views and activities. Many were former slave owners who had moved to the Queen City but continued to believe that African Americans were inferior to whites in every way. However, some people opposed slavery but believed that African Americans would move to the North and deprive white people of jobs. So to prevent Birney from printing his antislavery periodicals for a time, a mob of white Cincinnatians destroyed the newspaper's printing press on July 12, 1836. Despite this horrible act, Birney obtained another press, remained in the city, and continued to publish his periodical under great distress. (Courtesy of the Cincinnati Historical Society.)

Narrative of the Late Riotous Proceedings. During the 1830s, an Ohio Anti-Slavery Society branch was formed in Cincinnati with a biracial focus, that sought the immediate end of enslavement and rejected any colonization plan. (Courtesy of the National Underground Railroad Freedom Center.)

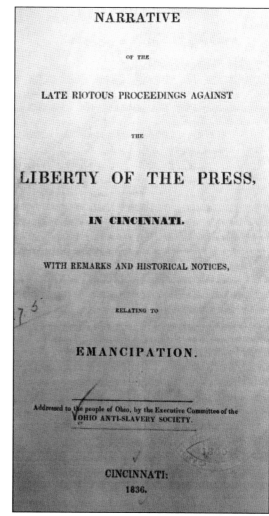

NARRATIVE

OF THE

LATE RIOTOUS PROCEEDINGS AGAINST

THE

LIBERTY OF THE PRESS,

IN CINCINNATI.

WITH REMARKS AND HISTORICAL NOTICES,

RELATING TO

EMANCIPATION.

Addressed to the people of Ohio, by the Executive Committee of the OHIO ANTI-SLAVERY SOCIETY.

CINCINNATI:
1836.

(17)

"A FUGITIVE FROM JUSTICE,"
$100 REWARD.

" The above sum will be paid for the delivery of one James G. Birney, a fugitive from justice, now abiding in the city of Cincinnati. Said Birney in all his associations and feelings is *black*; although his external appearance is white. The above reward will be paid and no questions asked by   OLD KENTUCKY.

James Birney, Fugitive from Justice. Numerous Cincinnatians were involved in harboring fugitives who had decided to escape the city. One of those individuals was James G. Birney. Upon his arrival in the city, Birney became a very active member of the Underground Railroad. In 1837, he was arrested and convicted of harboring a fugitive enslaved African American, but this decision was overturned by the Ohio Supreme Court. (Courtesy of the National Underground Railroad Freedom Center.)

ACHILLES H. PUGH. Born in Chester County, Pennsylvania, on March 10, 1805, Achilles Pugh and his family settled in Cadiz, Ohio, in 1809. In 1835, the Ohio Anti-Slavery Society was formed and Pugh quickly became supporter and later an editor of *The Philanthropist*. Because of various attacks, Pugh moved his press and paper to Springboro, Ohio. Pugh shipped the newspaper to Cincinnati on the Miami-Erie Canal. (Courtesy of the Ohio Historical Society.)

A.H. PUGH PRINTING COMPANY. Pugh was the founder of the A.H. Pugh Printing Company, a publishing firm located in Cincinnati. In April 1836, Pugh's company began publishing *The Philanthropist*. As a member of the Society of Friends, Pugh shared Birney's opposition to slavery. (Courtesy of the Cincinnati Historical Society.)

ANNA DONALDSON. Donaldson was one of the few women involved in the antislavery movement during the antebellum period. She and her two sons Christian and William moved to Avondale, a suburb of Cincinnati, in 1824. There, they gradually became involved in the inner workings of the antislavery movement. Although some of their neighbors were against such activities, the Donaldsons continued their abolitionist work for many years. (Courtesy of the New Richmond Historical Society.)

PRESBYTERIAN REFORM. The original Reformed Presbyterian (or Covenanter) Church of Cincinnati, which was reorganized in 1844, initially was established in 1810 and had been located in various parts of Pennsylvania and New York before coming to Cincinnati. By the mid-1830s, many members of its congregation had become abolitionists or active in the local Underground Railroad. Pictured here is Professor Willson of the Covenanter Church. (Courtesy of the Cincinnati Historical Society.)

CINCINNATI RACE RIOT OF 1841. Cincinnati's Fifth Street Market in 1840 symbolized the tranquil and pristine community life the city had emerged into from its inception early in the century. Many African Americans had traveled to the city in hopes of securing employment in the continuously expanding economic market. However, the entire atmosphere changed the following year. In 1841, the city experienced a powerful and deadly race riot that would be repeated several more times before the beginning of World War I. This specific conflict occurred after a long drought had created widespread unemployment in the city. Over a period of several days in September, unemployed white Cincinnatians attacked hundreds of local blacks, who fought back. As a result, African American Cincinnatians, some of whom had escaped from enslavement only a few weeks or months previously, were rounded up and jailed "for their own protection," according to the local authorities. (Courtesy of the Cincinnati Historical Society.)

LOCAL ANTISLAVERY SOCIETY'S LITERATURE. One of the main arguments used to justify the 1841 race riot was the belief that African Americans were inferior to whites and thus did not deserve to be recognized or protected by the legal system. However, the state and local antislavery societies organized a campaign to dispel this notion with a series of positive images. Pictured here is a pamphlet published by the Ohio Antislavery Society that shows the powerful work ethic that all African American Cincinnatians possessed. (Both, courtesy of the Cincinnati Historical Society.)

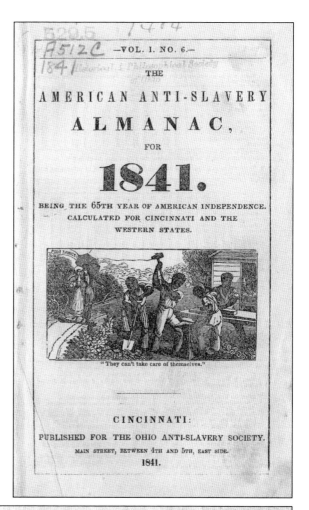

"They can't take care of themselves."

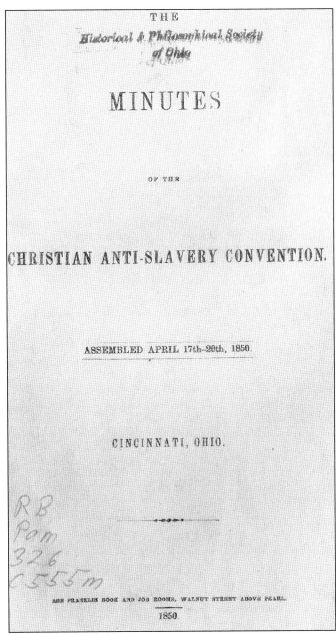

ANTISLAVERY CONVENTIONS. During the 1850s, a series of antislavery conventions and conferences were held in Cincinnati, which were attended by both well-known and obscure local and national leaders. The first was held in 1851 at a local church. One year later, in 1852, the speakers included a cadre of powerful local, regional, and national speakers who had obtained a great following, such as George Julian, Frederick Douglass, Henry Bibb, and John M. Langston. William Lloyd Garrison presided over the 1853 Cincinnati Convention. The public controversy that accompanied Garrison wherever he spoke resulted in extensive press coverage and large audiences in the city. By this time, Garrison had become one of the most sought out antislavery orators in the nation. His fiery prose could move most audiences in a matter of minutes. (Courtesy of the Cincinnati Historical Society.)

Three

THE UNDERGROUND RAILROAD BEGINS

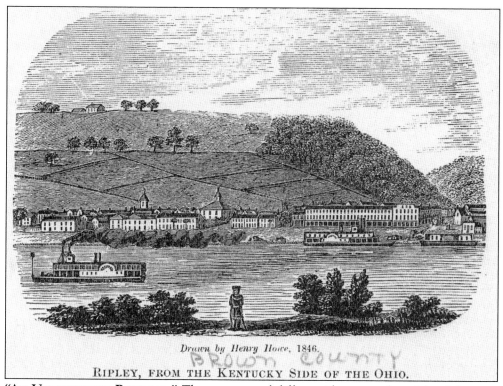

Drawn by Henry Howe, 1846.

BROWN COUNTY

RIPLEY, FROM THE KENTUCKY SIDE OF THE OHIO.

"AN UNDERGROUND RAILROAD." There are several different ideas as to the origin of the term "Underground Railroad." One of the most popular interpretations is that in 1831, a fugitive slave named Tice Davids escaped from Kentucky to a safe-house in Sandusky, Ohio. When Davids's owner could not locate him after a long day of searching in Ripley, Ohio (pictured), he angrily proclaimed, "The nigger must have gone off on an underground railroad." (Courtesy of the Cincinnati Historical Society.)

PRES. GEORGE WASHINGTON. George Washington owned hundreds of enslaved African Americans. More importantly, when a talented personal servant ran away from Mount Vernon in 1797, Washington expressed great surprise and subsequently noted that many enslaved African Americans probably had escaped from their owners during the previous decade. (Courtesy of the Library of Congress.)

A RUNAWAY SLAVE ADVERTISEMENT. Young men ran away in greater numbers because they often were not married, or if married, they had not yet begun a family. Those who were married sometimes took their families with them, but in most cases they did not and thus were forced to leave their wives and children behind. Young men also ran away more often because they were more willing to defy their owners. (Courtesy of the Ohio Historical Society.)

EMILY. Compared to their male cohorts, young enslaved women were less likely to run away because they had often begun to raise families by their late teens and early twenties. They were unwilling to leave children behind or take them on the dangerous journey. However, some enslaved women did decide to take on the challenge, such as 17-year-old Emily, described here. (Courtesy of the Ohio Historical Society.)

100 DOLLARS
REWARD!

Ranaway from the subscriber on the **27th** of July, my Black Woman, named

EMILY,

Seventeen years of age, well grown, black color, has a whining voice. She took with her one dark calico and one blue and white dress, a red corded gingham bonnet; a white striped shawl and slippers. I will pay the above reward if taken near the Ohio river on the Kentucky side, or **THREE HUNDRED DOLLARS**, if taken in the State of Ohio, and delivered to me near Lewisburg, Mason County, Ky. **THO'S. H. WILLIAMS.**
August 4, 1853.

IMAGE OF SLAVE AUCTION BY CHARLES WEBER. One of the primary motives for enslaved African Americans to abscond, and which caused a cadre of individuals to participant in Underground Railroad activities, was the buying and selling of persons of African descent at the auction block. These auctions took place regularly across the Ohio River in Covington, Kentucky. (Courtesy of the Cincinnati Historical Society.)

ESCAPING VIA THE UNDERGROUND RAILROAD. We may never know the exact number of people who escaped through the Underground Railroad, but the origins, development, and use of the network must be placed within the larger context of the increasing southern white violence against African American families, slave resistance, and the expansion of aggressive northern abolitionists. (Courtesy of the Ohio Historical Society.)

PEOPLE HELPING PEOPLE. The escape of thousands of enslaved persons via the Underground Railroad was by no means a passive act. All involved parties had to participant in various activities such as raising money to pay for the escapees' transportation, recruiting and helping other escapees, and locating places to stay. This was not an easy journey and thus, Underground Railroad work was both risky and dangerous. (Courtesy of the Ohio Historical Society.)

THE RANKIN FAMILY. One of the most prominent families involved in Underground Railroad activities in the Cincinnati region was the Rankin family. Led by Rev. John Rankin, who was born in 1793 in Tennessee, the Rankin family's assault against the system of human bondage was originated by John Rankin's mother, who made her views on the topic very well known to all the members of the family throughout her 82 years of life. Adam Rankin, the oldest of John's children, recalled how his grandmother's antislavery stance affected his life for many years. John also proclaimed his antislavery views early in his life, specifically through a series of powerful letters to his brother that later became an inspiration to national abolitionists such as William Lloyd Garrison, Frederick Douglass, and James G. Birney. (Courtesy of the Ohio Historical Society.)

HENRY "BOX" BROWN. Henry Brown was born into enslavement 1815 in Louisa County, Virginia. In 1848, his wife, who was owned by another master and who was pregnant with their fourth child, was sold away to North Carolina, along with their children. Soon after, Brown developed an escape plan with the help of a free black American, who conspired to ship him in a box to Philadelphia. (Courtesy of the Library of Congress.)

ELLEN AND WILLIAM CRAFT. In 1848, Ellen and William Craft developed a secret plan to escape from the system of human bondage in Macon, Georgia. The daughter of an African American woman and a white owner, Ellen, who looked white, dressed in clothes that made her look like a slave-owner, while her husband, William, appeared as Ellen's enslaved African American. The two of them packed some bags, left their plantation, headed north, and became involved in the abolition movement. (Courtesy of the Library of Congress.)

HIDING PLACES FOR RUNAWAYS. The dream of freedom in the North or in Canada, the so-called "Promised Land," went unfulfilled for thousands of runaways. However, a few runaways traveling at night or hiding aboard sailing vessels as well as in safe-houses, made it. Those who were lucky enough to escape concealed themselves, used various disguises, obtained free papers, and traveled the back roads to gain their freedom. (Courtesy of the Ohio Historical Society.)

ESCAPING VIA INLAND WATERWAYS. On foot, runaways seldom traveled more than 10 to 15 miles per night. Another way, however, in which runaways absconded was through the use of various creeks and small streams that fed into a larger waterway, especially in the northern Kentucky and southwest Ohio regions. Pictured here is one example. (Courtesy of the Cincinnati Historical Society.)

THE IMPORTANCE OF ASSISTANCE. Very few successful escapes planned in Kentucky for an individual or a group of people to reach Ohio were completed unaided. Even when one decided to use water vessels, such as boats or steamships, accurate information and assistance from several individuals was needed. (Courtesy of the Cincinnati Historical Society.)

USING WAGONS TO ESCAPE. Ten of thousands of enslaved African Americans absconded to various towns and cities, seeking safe havens as well as anonymity and isolation. Cities that were located by waterways, like Cincinnati, Pittsburgh, or Detroit, offered opportunities for runaways to hide their identities, create new ones, and move throughout the region and beyond via carts, buggies, wagons, horses. (Courtesy of the Cincinnati Historical Society.)

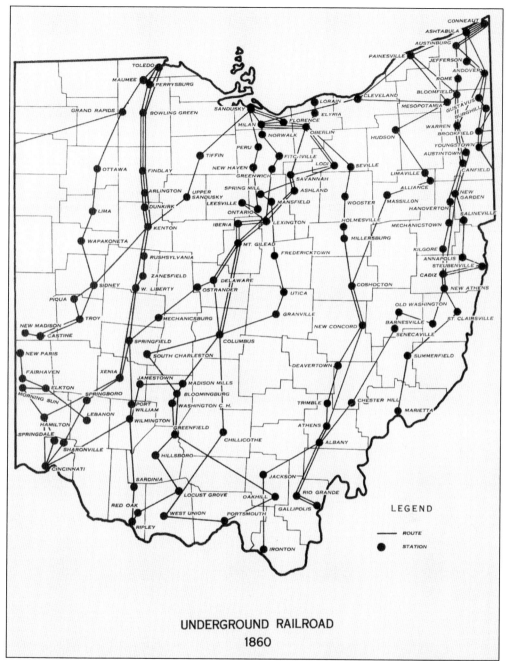

UNDERGROUND RAILROAD
1860

THE UNDERGROUND RAILROAD IN OHIO. Despite the impossibility of open communication and outward coordination, the Underground Railroad in Ohio was an amazingly efficient, effective, and organized operation. Routes through the forests, farms, towns, and cities were established from one hiding place to the next. In all, nearly 3,000 miles of routes were established across the state, most bound in a northeasterly direction, along with at least 23 points of entry along the Ohio River. (Courtesy of the Ohio Historical Society.)

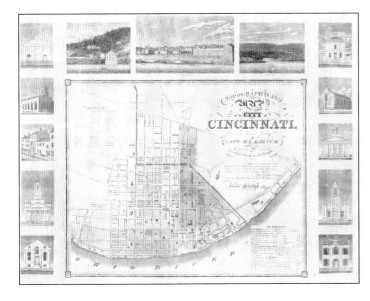

CINCINNATI IN 1830. During the 1830s in Cincinnati, individuals such as John Mercer Langston, Lyman Beecher, Levi Coffin, Frances Scroggins Brown, Thomas Woodson, and Allen Temple, as well as organizations like the Ohio Antislavery Society, helped to foster an environment where thousands of fugitive African Americans found a safe haven. (Courtesy of the Cincinnati Historical Society.)

BOATS DOCKED IN CINCINNATI. Enslaved African Americans often escaped from or through Kentucky by using the waterways. The motives and actions of fugitive African Americans and those who assisted them cannot be interpreted, evaluated, or analyzed in any great detail outside of this context. The locations, landscape, and environment, as well as the mountains, rivers, and roads, were very important during the various escape attempts, especially in the Cincinnati region. (Courtesy of the Cincinnati Historical Society.)

FUGITIVES AND FREE AFRICAN AMERICANS IN CINCINNATI. During the 1830s and 1840s, many African American residents of Cincinnati found themselves on the front line of the struggle against American enslavement. Like their brothers and sisters along the Ohio River east and west of Cincinnati, these individuals made up a beachhead of freedom. To hide their true status, enslaved people would often find themselves working in the streets of Cincinnati. Some of them were rented out and worked within the city. Others were brought into the city by their owners for business and vacations. These various situations allowed the enslaved people to have access to those folks who assisted other fugitives to move in the city and into the local free African American community with little resistance. These areas varied in size and population throughout the antebellum period. Pictured here is a view of downtown Cincinnati in the 1830s. (Courtesy of the Cincinnati Historical Society.)

EMERGING AFRICAN AMERICAN COMMUNITY. Despite the intent of the Black Law of Ohio that sought to restrict the migration of fugitive African Americans to the Buckeye state, thousands came, especially to the growing city of Cincinnati. Before 1820, the communities of African Americans in Cincinnati depended mostly on free blacks, African American fugitives, and freed persons of color to increase their population. Furthermore, Cincinnati's location on the edge of the system of enslavement, just across the Ohio River, meant that many African Americans lived under the constant threat of kidnappers and slave catchers. Despite the possibility of an escape, slaves frequently were sent into the city alone on errands or to buy dry goods, fruit, and other wares at the market. Some were granted passes to attend one of the black churches in the city or to work in various capacities. Pictured here is a view of downtown Cincinnati in the 1830s. (Courtesy of the Cincinnati Historical Society.)

BUCKTOWN. Soon after Cincinnati was founded in 1788, free and enslaved African Americans came across the Ohio River to live and work in the city. Many had been born free, some were freed slaves, and others were fugitives who had escaped their masters and plantations in the South. Although the Northwest Ordinance of 1787 prohibited slavery in the North and west of the Ohio River, the Ohio Legislature passed the Black Laws in 1803 and 1807 to restrict the opportunities of the region's African American residents. But because of the city's bustling riverfront and growing economy, work was plentiful and laws were sometimes ignored or selectively enforced. As a result, the city's African American population began to gradually increase. However, when it rose to large numbers in 1829, a white mob attacked hundreds of African American homes in Bucktown, causing over 1,000 African Americans to leave Cincinnati for settlements in northern Ohio or Canada. (Courtesy of the Cincinnati Historical Society.)

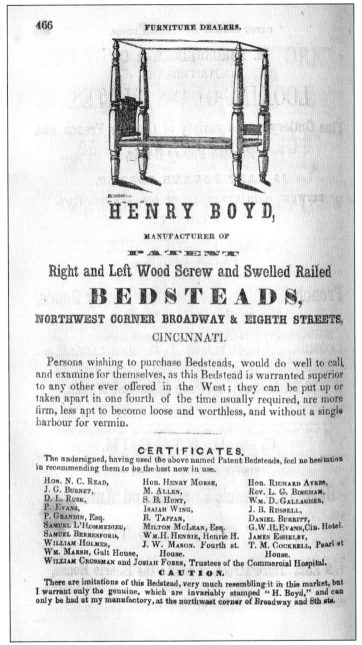

HENRY BOYD,

MANUFACTURER OF

PATENT

Right and Left Wood Screw and Swelled Railed

BEDSTEADS,

NORTHWEST CORNER BROADWAY & EIGHTH STREETS,

CINCINNATI.

Persons wishing to purchase Bedsteads, would do well to call and examine for themselves, as this Bedstead is warranted superior to any other ever offered in the West; they can be put up or taken apart in one fourth of the time usually required, are more firm, less apt to become loose and worthless, and without a single harbour for vermin.

CERTIFICATES.

The undersigned, having used the above named Patent Bedsteads, feel no hesitation in recommending them to be the best now in use.

Hon. N. C. Read,	Hon. Henry Morse,	Hon. Richard Ayres,
J. G. Burnet,	M. Allen,	Rev. L. G. Bingham,
D. L. Rusk,	S. B. Hunt,	Wm. D. Gallagher,
P. Evans,	Isaiah Wing,	J. B. Russell,
P. Grandin, Esq.	B. Tappan,	Daniel Burritt,
Samuel L'Hommedieu,	Milton McLean, Esq.	G.W.H.Evans,Cin. Hotel.
Samuel Berresford,	Wm.H. Henrie, Henrie H.	James Eshelby,
William Holmes,	J. W. Mason. Fourth st.	T. M. Cockrell, Pearl st
Wm. Marsh, Galt House,	House.	House.

William Crossman and Josiah Fobes, Trustees of the Commercial Hospital.

CAUTION.

There are imitations of this Bedstead, very much resembling it in this market, but I warrant only the genuine, which are invariably stamped "H. Boyd," and can only be had at my manufactory, at the northwest corner of Broadway and 8th sts.

HENRY BOYD. Born into slavery in Kentucky in 1802, Henry Boyd became a skilled carpenter and was able to purchase his freedom in 1826 when he was 24 years old. He relocated to Cincinnati and began his new life as a house builder. Boyd eventually earned enough money to purchase the freedom of his brother and sister. In 1836, he established the H. Boyd Company and began to make and sell his invention, called the Boyd Bedstead. As a very successful member of the African American community in the Queen City, by the mid-1830s, Boyd had amassed a wealth of about $3,000 and employed several workers. A decade and a half later, he had accumulated an enormous fortune of about $420,000. Boyd used most of his wealth to buy numerous African Americans out of bondage. (Courtesy of the Cincinnati Historical Society.)

THE *DISFRANCHISED AMERICAN*. During the antebellum years, black Cincinnatians developed mutual aid societies, fraternal clubs, and the Colored Orphan Asylum as essential organizations to uplift the entire race. These entities lent themselves to the goal of racial uplift because the local African American community hoped to obtain racial independence and self-sufficiency in a city that had turned its back on African Americans for many decades. One of the ways in which these objectives were communicated to other black Americans was through a prominent newspaper known as the *Disfranchised American*. This was the first African American newspaper published in Cincinnati, which was only published for one year, 1843–1844. However, the editors included several prominent community leaders such as Alphonso M. Sumner, William E. Yancy, Rev. Thomas Woodson, Gideon Q. Langton, and Owen T.B. Nickens. (Courtesy of the Cincinnati Historical Society.)

SAMUEL AND SALLY HOUSE. In 1847, Samuel and Sally Wilson, a very active and important married abolitionist team, bought several acres of land and a small cabin from Freeman Cary, who resided in College Hill. Their daughter, Mary Jane, was one of the first teachers at the Ohio Female College; their two sons attended Cary Academy. All the members of the Wilson family were involved in the origin and development of the Underground Railroad in the area. Indeed, the house in which Samuel and Sally resided was used a safe house for at least four years for the hundreds of fugitive African Americans who had escaped the South and traveled to Cincinnati or parts north looking for freedom. (Courtesy of the Cincinnati Historical Society.)

COLORED SCHOOL SYSTEM. In 1852, nine years prior to the beginning of the Civil War, several thousand African American Cincinnatians successfully moved to create their own separate public school system. At this time, the state of Ohio granted them the right to create and operate the Independent Colored School System. Financed by proceeds from taxes on property owned by local African Americans and operated by a board elected by the same residents, this school system was credited with providing a base for Cincinnati's emerging black middle class. More importantly, the emergence of this educational system and the accompanying Colored School Board of Cincinnati made the venture one of the few independent black educational systems in the nation. Two of the most important individuals who led the battle to create the city's "colored" school system were Peter H. Clark and John I. Gaines. (Courtesy of Richard Cooper.)

MEETING IN THE AFRICAN CHURCH, CINCINNATI, OHIO.

FAMILIES AND COMMUNITIES. During the antebellum period, Cincinnati began to emerge as a force in the manufacturing industry and became the nation's leader in pork packing and steamboat construction. The city's economic growth also occurred as a result of the region's ability to supply much-needed manufactured goods for most of the southern and western parts of the United States, which caused it to earn the name "Queen City of the West." As a result, thousands of individuals from various ethnic backgrounds and racial groups flocked to the city seeking jobs and other economic opportunities. In less than 50 years, Cincinnati transformed itself from a small village to a booming city that rivaled several more established Midwestern and East Coast cities. The population of African Americans in the city also increased to about 3,000, which made it one of the 10 largest free black communities in the nation at the time. (Courtesy of the Cincinnati Historical Society.)

Four

ROUTES AND STATIONS

ALLEN TEMPLE. As one of the oldest African American churches in Cincinnati, Allen Temple African Methodist Episcopal Bethel dates to 1808, when it was initially organized as Mill Creek Church. Because of its continuous connection to the wellbeing of fugitive African Americans, the church was burned down several times between 1812 and 1815. Nevertheless, Allen Temple continued to assist runaways until the end of the Civil War. (Courtesy of the Cincinnati Historical Society.)

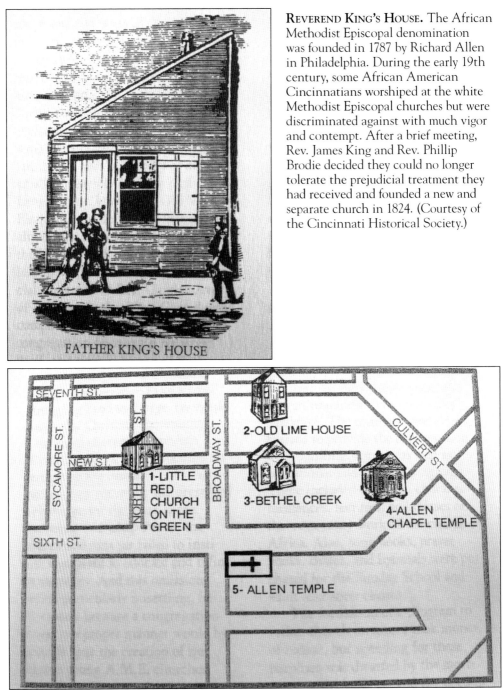

FATHER KING'S HOUSE

REVEREND KING'S HOUSE. The African Methodist Episcopal denomination was founded in 1787 by Richard Allen in Philadelphia. During the early 19th century, some African American Cincinnatians worshiped at the white Methodist Episcopal churches but were discriminated against with much vigor and contempt. After a brief meeting, Rev. James King and Rev. Phillip Brodie decided they could no longer tolerate the prejudicial treatment they had received and founded a new and separate church in 1824. (Courtesy of the Cincinnati Historical Society.)

CHURCH LOCATIONS. Because of the church's continuous growth and the increase in vandalism at Allen Temple, the congregation was forced to seek another location. In 1870, the congregation bought the former Bene Israel Synagogue at 538 Broadway Street, a larger and more secure facility with barred windows and an iron fence. After satisfying their debts, the congregation refocused and began to work for social welfare, stability, and the uplifting of the local African American community. (Courtesy of the Cincinnati Historical Society.)

CALVARY METHODIST CHURCH.
In the tradition of numerous
African American churches
during the antebellum period,
the Calvary Methodist Church
of Cincinnati not only helped
local African Americans
with their spiritual needs and
wants, but was also part of
the black community that
provided economic and social
opportunities for thousands
of black Americans. Several
members of Calvary Methodist
were involved in assisting
numerous individuals gain their
freedom via the Underground
Railroad. (Courtesy of the
Cincinnati Historical Society.)

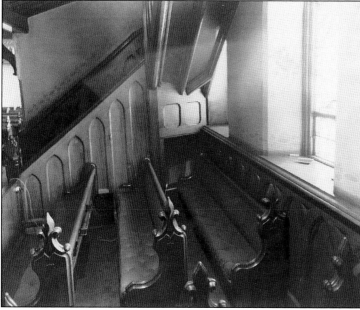

**CALVARY METHODIST
INTERIOR.** The
importance of
Calvary Methodist
Church continued
until after the Civil
War ended in 1865.
During the post–Civil
War years, it was
discovered that the
church contained
numerous secret halls
and rooms where
individuals could
hide. (Courtesy of
the Ohio Historical
Society.)

UNITARIAN CHURCH. Looking West from Vine Street along Fourth Street in the mid-1850s, this image shows one of the original locations of the First Unitarian Church of Cincinnati. First Unitarian Church is a historic congregation of the Unitarian Universalist Association. Founded in the early 19th century, it survived a series of divisions and reunifications, particularly over the topic of slavery. (Courtesy of the Cincinnati Historical Society.)

UNION BAPTIST CHURCH. Established on July 21, 1831, Union Baptist Church, the second oldest African American church in the state of Ohio, was founded to foster religious freedom for local African Americans. With the system of enslavement weighing heavily on many of the members of the congregation, the church started monthly prayer meetings in 1839 to pray for the end of this terrible institution. (Courtesy of the National Underground Railroad Freedom Center.)

UNION BAPTIST CHURCH 1855 RECORDS.
During its early years, Union Baptist
Church was involved in numerous other
projects such as missionary trips to other
parts of Ohio and to Africa. Since its
inception, Union Baptist Church has
also been known for its vocal opposition
to slavery. This position was tested
when an African American fugitive
appeared at the door of Union Baptist
requesting that the leaders of the church
buy him out of enslavement. During
the antebellum years, Union Baptist set
up a fund to help African American
runaways. (Both, courtesy of the National
Underground Railroad Freedom Center.)

WESLEY CHAPEL CHURCH. Built in 1831 on the north side of Fifth Street between Broadway and Sycamore Streets, Wesley Chapel Church was a Methodist congregation. It was a simple red brick Georgian structure copied after John Wesley's original Methodist church in London. With a seating capacity of 1,200, during the antebellum period Wesley Chapel was the largest indoor meeting facility west of the Alleghenies and the largest building in Cincinnati for many years. In 1841, the funeral of Pres. William Henry Harrison was held there. In 1845, former president John Quincy Adams spoke at the facility in honor of the newly constructed Cincinnati Observatory, which was located in the Mount Adams part of the city. Both before and during the Civil War, several antislavery political meetings and rallies were held at Wesley Chapel because of its central location. Some of the church members in later years became actively involved in Underground Railroad activities. In 1972, the church was demolished and a new church built at 80 East McMicken Avenue. (Courtesy of the Cincinnati Historical Society.)

ZION BAPTIST CHURCH. Zion Baptist Church was organized in 1842 by Father Wallace Shelton along with several members of the Union Baptist Church of Cincinnati. The congregation was initially located on Plum Street. From this location, many members of the church actively participated in Underground Railroad activities. (Courtesy of the Cincinnati Historical Society.)

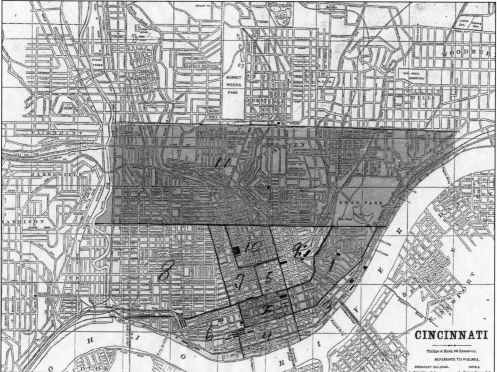

LITTLE AFRICA. During the antebellum period, one of main areas in which black Cincinnatians migrated to organize themselves was Little Africa. The areas were not "ghettoes," but instead were very livable residential communities. This region was located on Fourth Street, which at the time was along the waterfront. Pictured here is an 1850 ward map that highlights this African American community. (Courtesy of the Cincinnati Historical Society.)

ENTRANCE TO REAR COURT OF BUCK TOWN.

BUCKTOWN. During the 1830s and 1840s, another significant group of African Americans lived in the first ward, between Main and Broadway Streets just south of Sixth Street in an area known as Bucktown. This region contained not only thousands of African Americans, but also a number of black-owned businesses and churches. Several illegal and underground industries also operated in Bucktown. (Courtesy of the Cincinnati Historical Society.)

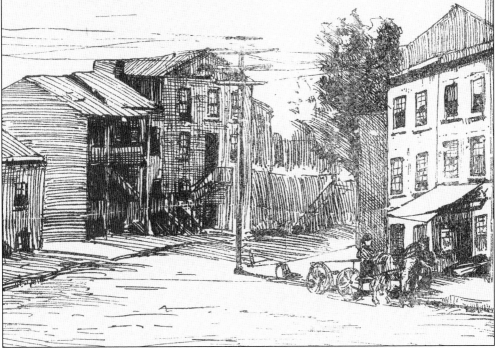

SKETCH OF BUCKTOWN. The importance of Bucktown for black Cincinnatians has received little attention from most historians. Its location on the riverfront made it a primary location for many fugitives. However, several hundred free blacks also lived in this same neighborhood. Both groups helped to create a vibrant and powerful community. (Courtesy of the Cincinnati Historical Society.)

UNDERGROUND RAILROAD STATION IN BUCKTOWN. Not only was Bucktown one of the two major black communities in Cincinnati during the antebellum period, the neighborhood was also known as an important destination for runaways as it had various churches and homes that were key stops on the Underground Railroad. (Courtesy of the Ohio Historical Society.)

UNDERGROUND RAILROAD STATION. An examination of the history of African Americans in Cincinnati proves that the Underground Railroad was not built on the backs of individuals but on the shoulders of communities. Indeed, the Underground Railroad in Cincinnati was characterized by a community-wide network and various patterns of cooperation that aimed to assist runaway African Americans. Pictured here is one example of a facility that was linked to the Underground Railroad in the city. (Courtesy of the Ohio Historical Society.)

THE DUMAS HOUSE. The Dumas House was a black-owned boarding home located in downtown Cincinnati that doubled as a way station for fugitive slaves. The Dumas House was a popular lodging place for African American visitors to the city, enslaved or free. While it is difficult to determine whether the owners actively or passively harbored these fugitives, the Dumas House was a prominent station on the Underground Railroad. (Courtesy of the Cincinnati Historical Society.)

CANALS. Fugitives could not escape from Kentucky without crossing the Ohio River. Because no bridges were built until after the Civil War, the river could only be crossed by boats, on foot if the river was frozen, or by swimming. There also were several local canals and streams that fed into the Ohio River. Many used their positions as laborers on these waterways to abscond. Indeed, a nearby waterway granted a fugitive a great ready-made escape route, at least initially. Hundreds of enslaved persons used canals and streams to initiate or continue their movement to the North to freedom. (Both, courtesy of the Cincinnati Historical Society.)

JOHN RANDOLPH. The first major African-American migration came to the Miami Valley and Piqua, Ohio, region around 1847, when the manumitted slaves of John Randolph settled in the counties of Miami and Shelby, in Rossville, Ohio, just across the Great Miami River. Initially, Randolph (a distant cousin of Thomas Jefferson) had been one of the largest owners of enslaved African Americans in Virginia. Upon his death, however, he requested in his will that all of his slaves be freed. However, his brother contested the will. As a result, it was not until 13 years later, in 1847, that Randolph's enslaved African Americans were set free. Soon after obtaining their freedom, most of Randolph's freedmen formed a "wagon train" and headed to Cincinnati. Once there, they traveled farther north to Piqua, where the atmosphere of racial oppression was apparently less than what they found in Cincinnati. (Courtesy of the Ohio Historical Society.)

COLLEGE HILL. College Hill, Ohio, was settled in 1813. Today, it is one of the most vibrant of Cincinnati's 52 neighborhoods. It is located a few miles north of downtown within the 3.4 square miles on the northern edge of the city. The neighborhood is home to a diverse mix of families and singles, young and old. During the antebellum period, this region became a major stop on the Underground Railroad. (Courtesy of the Cincinnati Historical Society.)

THE ZEBULON STRONG HOME. Located on Hamilton Avenue, this residence was the private home of Zebulon Strong, an abolitionist who was part of the local and regional antislavery movement. This facility was one of two residences Strong used to harbor fugitive African Americans. Runaways would come up the east ravine near a railroad line, and hide in the nearby forest until dark, then continue their journey north. While the fugitives were hiding, the Strong children would play in the area and leave food and drink without any witnesses. On some occasions, Strong used his own wagon to help African Americans who had absconded. (Courtesy of Richard Cooper.)

BEHIND THE ZEBULON STRONG HOME. Behind the Strongs' home were wooded areas rarely used by locals. During the antebellum years, a very important secret route was discovered by some old farmers. Initially, they rarely spoke about seeing fugitives running through or sleeping in the area. However, the situation changed when the Fugitive Slave Act of 1850 was passed and the recapture of runaways became more lucrative. Shown here is a wooded pathway and waterway in that many enslaved African Americans traveled along and through on their way north. (Both, courtesy of Richard Cooper.)

CINCINNATI'S NEW ORPHAN ASYLUM FOR COLORED CHILDREN. This organization was started in 1844 by Lydia P. Mott and several other African American and white leaders. The organization initially consisted of six white men, ten African American men, four white women, and eight African American women. Among the six white men was Salmon P. Chase, a local attorney who later argued some of the most important cases on racial relations in the nation. In 1845, Chase helped to secure the organization's first charter with the state of Ohio and the orphanage opened its doors in a building located on Ninth Street, between Elm and Plum Streets. When the asylum slipped into bad repair during the early 1850s due to a lack of funding, Levi and Catherine Coffin, two whites who were associated with local and regional Underground Railroad activities, took over the facilities for a few years and helped the organization return to prominence. (Courtesy of the Cincinnati Historical Society.)

GLENDALE. Incorporated in 1855, Glendale, Ohio, is a northern suburb of Cincinnati with a land area of 1.7 square miles and a population of 2,155. This village 12 miles north of Cincinnati once was a series of fine farms, amounting to 565 acres. It is located on the Cincinnati, Hamilton & Dayton Railroad. During the antebellum period, Glendale played a very prominent and important role in the origin and development of the Underground Railroad in Cincinnati and the Midwest at large. John W. Van Zandt and his church were located in Glendale. It also is well known that many enslaved people were hidden throughout the Glendale/Sharonville area. (Courtesy of the Cincinnati Historical Society.)

JOHN VAN ZANDT. This Hamilton Country, Ohio, farmer was a former slave owner who had a vivid dream one night and decided to free his slaves. He moved to Ohio and became an ordained minister at a church in Glendale. (Courtesy of the Clifton Waller Barrett Library of American Literature, Special Collections, University of Virginia Library, Charlottesville.)

VAN ZANDT GRAVE SITE. While living in Evendale, Ohio, just north of Cincinnati, Van Zandt regularly harbored fugitives in the basement of his house and helped them escape to Canada. During the 1840s, he was caught while involved in these activities. He was excommunicated from the Methodist Episcopal Church, which had already joined the southern portion of the national congregations. (Courtesy of Richard Cooper.)

Five

FRIENDS FOR FUGITIVE AFRICAN AMERICANS

CHARLES T. WEBBER PAINTING OF LEVI COFFIN, 1891. *The Underground Railroad*, painted by Charles T. Webber for the 1893 World's Columbian Exposition, celebrates abolitionists' efforts to end slavery. It depicts Levi Coffin; his wife, Catharine Coffin; and Hannah Haddock, all friends of the artist, leading a group of fugitive slaves to freedom on a winter morning. The setting of the painting may be the Coffin farm in Cincinnati. (Courtesy of the Ohio Historical Society.)

CATHERINE COFFIN. Born in Guilford County, North Carolina, in 1803, Catherine was the daughter of Stanton and Mary White. In 1824, she married long-time friend Levi. Their marriage ceremony was held in the Hopewell Friends Meetinghouse in North Carolina. Catherine's family is believed to have been involved in helping hundreds of enslaved African Americans escape from bondage. (Courtesy of the Cincinnati Historical Society.)

LEVI COFFIN. Coffin was born in New Garden, Guilford County, in 1789. In 1821, he and his cousin, Vestal Coffin, organized a school for enslaved African Americans and taught them to read by using the Bible. Coffin's involvement in helping numerous runaways earned him the honorary title of "president" of the Underground Railroad. (Courtesy of the Cincinnati Historical Society.)

THE COFFIN HOME. To thousands of escapees, this eight-room brick home in Newport (Fountain City), Indiana, became a safe haven on their journey north. Levi and Catharine Coffin, two North Carolina Quakers who opposed slavery, moved to Indiana during the 1820s. During the 20 years they lived in Newport, the Coffins helped more than 2,000 slaves reach safety. (Courtesy of the Cincinnati Historical Society.)

THE COFFIN BUSINESS. In 1847, Coffin moved to the Cincinnati area, where he took over the management of a local business. He rented out his Newport, Indiana, business before leaving the state. Coffin's Cincinnati business became one of the first "Fair Trade" facilities in the nation, selling goods produced without the use of any slave labor. (Courtesy of the Cincinnati Historical Society.)

EDWARD HARWOOD, W.H. BRISBANE, AND LEVI COFFIN. All three of these men were pioneering abolitionists who helped to transform the attack on the system of human bondage during the antebellum years. They not only published papers and made numerous public lectures on the subject, they also were involved in the development of the Underground Railroad. (Courtesy of the Ohio Historical Society.)

NORTON S. TOWNSHEND. Born in Northamptonshire, England, in 1830, Townshend emigrated to the United States with his parents, who settled in Avon, Ohio. In 1837, Townshend became acquainted with Salmon P. Chase of Cincinnati when he was attending medical school. The two men began to assist each other in helping individuals escape through the Underground Railroad in the Cincinnati area. (Courtesy of the Ohio Historical Society.)

GAMALIEL BAILEY. Born in Mount Holly, New Jersey, in 1807, Bailey moved with his family to Philadelphia at the age of nine. In 1827, he graduated from the Jefferson Medical College in Philadelphia and subsequently moved to Baltimore. In 1831, he moved to Cincinnati, where he set up a medical practice and began to lecture on physiology at the Lane Theological Seminary and soon became an ardent abolitionist. (Courtesy of the Ohio Historical Society.)

RUTHERFORD B. HAYES. Hayes was born in 1822 in Delaware, Ohio. After graduating from Kenyon College in 1842 and attending Harvard Law School in 1845, Hayes began a law practice in Cincinnati. In 1876 he became the 19th president of the United States and helped to shape the political and racial landscape of the country during the Reconstruction Era. (Courtesy of the Library of Congress.)

ADAM LOWRY RANKIN. Adam Lowry Rankin was born November 4, 1816, in Jonesboro, Tennessee. The oldest of John and Jean Rankin's 13 children, Adam carried on his parents' crusading work against slavery. His life changed from his earlier dream of a career in carpentry when he visited a ship docked in Ripley and saw the misery of captured runaways. From that point forward, he vowed to "fight slavery until it was dead." Soon after he made this statement, Rankin began to study for the ministry and enrolled in Lane Seminary in Cincinnati, where he guided runaway slaves to stations north of the city, often to Wilmington, Ohio. Rankin made these secret trips in the evening, returning for classes in the morning. In all, he is estimated to have helped some 300 runaways on their way to free lives. (Courtesy of the Ohio Historical Society.)

LAURA HAVILAND. Laura S. Smith was born a Quaker in Leeds County, Ontario, Canada, in 1808 to Americans Daniel Smith and Asenath "Sene" Blancher, who had emigrated shortly before her birth. In 1815, she and her family moved to the town of Cambria in western New York. At this time, there was no formal educational facility in the area, so she was home-schooled by her mother for the next six years. At the age of 16, young Laura met Charles Haviland Jr., a devout Quaker whose parents were respected local ministers. In 1825, they were married in Lockport, New York. Together they organized an active Underground Railroad network that ventured into Michigan. In 1837, Haviland started an integrated school for black and white children known as the Raisin Institute. Working to end slavery most of her adult life, Haviland spent her free time teaching, including for several years in Cincinnati. (Courtesy of the Ohio Historical Society.)

PETER H. CLARK. Peter H. Clark was born in Cincinnati in 1829 to Michael Clark, a local barber, while his mother was one of Clark's enslaved African Americans. In 1846, Clark became a teacher in an African American school in Cincinnati. He considered education essential for the improvement of the African American condition and a major force in forging a path for full and equal citizenship for each and every black American, not only in Cincinnati but in the nation at large. After the death of his father in 1849, Clark took over his barbershop and decided to break with local custom and run an "equal rights" shop, which led to complaints from white customers that caused Clark to leave the profession. Several years later, he moved to New Orleans, where he found work as a clerk. He held that job until 1852, when he came back to Cincinnati and became a school principal, where he remained for more than three decades. (Courtesy of the Cincinnati Historical Society.)

PETER STILL. Peter Still, the brother of William Still, had been an enslaved African for about 40 years and was able to save $500 to purchase his freedom. Assisted by a trusted Jewish sympathizer named Joseph Friedman, Still made his way to Philadelphia, where he received permission from a local African American church to post notices that he was searching for his mother, whom he had not seen since he was six years old. Miraculously, he was interviewed by his own brother, William Still, whom he had never known. After Peter experienced the joy of reuniting with his biological brother, he turned his focus to attempting to raise $5,000 to free his wife and three children in Alabama. (Courtesy of the Library of Congress.)

HARRIET BEECHER STOWE. Born in 1811 in Litchfield, Connecticut, where her father, Rev. Lyman Beecher, was a leading Congregational minister, Harriet Beecher Stowe gradually began to question the system of human bondage. In 1832, Harriet moved to Cincinnati when her father became the head of Lane Theological Seminary. However, it was Harriet who became the most famous Beecher upon the publication of her book, *Uncle Tom's Cabin*, which was originally serialized in the abolitionist newspaper *The National Era* from 1851 to 1852. The novel moved thousands of northerners to tears and made the system of human bondage more personal to them. (Courtesy of the Cincinnati Historical Society.)

HARRIET BEECHER STOWE'S FAMILY HOME IN WALNUT HILLS, OHIO. This was once the residence of Harriet Beecher Stowe. In 1832, young Harriet and her family moved to Cincinnati when her father, a Congregationalist minister, accepted an offer to teach at the Lane Seminary. Both the home and the seminary became a central point for the emerging abolition movement of the antebellum period. (Courtesy of the Cincinnati Historical Society.)

THE "EDGEMONT INN." The Edgemont Inn is a two-story gray painted brick building on the corner of Gilbert and Foraker Avenues. Before becoming the Edgemont Inn, this was another home in which Harriet Beecher Stowe and her family lived during their time in Cincinnati. Numerous local, regional, and national abolitionists visited the family regularly throughout the antebellum period. (Courtesy of the Ohio Historical Society.)

THE LONDON VERSION OF *UNCLE TOM'S CABIN.* Harriet Beecher Stowe published her famous novel in 1852; it became one the best-selling novels of the 19th century. It also is credited with starting the nation's movement toward the Civil War during the later decades of the antebellum era. Three years after it was published, in 1855, it was still called by many "the most popular novel of our day." Even President Lincoln noted the impact of the book. It also helped to popularize numerous stereotypical racist images such as the "mammy," the "pickaninny," and the "Uncle Tom." (Both, courtesy of the Cincinnati Historical Society.)

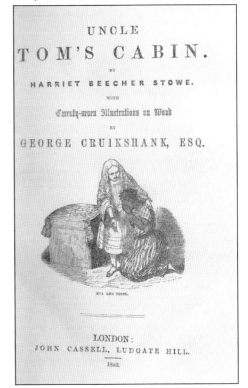

POSTER ADVERTISEMENT FOR UNCLE TOM'S CABIN. Stowe was partly inspired to write and publish *Uncle Tom's Cabin* after she read the 1849 slave narrative *The Life of Josiah Henson, Formerly a Slave, Now an Inhabitant of Canada, as Narrated by Himself.* Henson had lived and worked on a tobacco plantation in North Bethesda, Maryland, owned by Isaac Riley. In 1830, he escaped and traveled to Ontario, Canada, where he helped other fugitive African Americans settle and become self-sufficient. Henson also wrote his memoirs when he was living in Canada. Stowe's book received much more attention mainly because of the publisher's massive advertising campaign. (Courtesy of the Cincinnati Historical Society.)

JAY RIAL'S IDEAL FROM STOWE'S UNCLE TOM'S CABIN. Harriet Beecher Stowe said she based *Uncle Tom's Cabin* on a variety of interviews with people who had escaped the system of human bondage and migrated to Cincinnati. The book opens with a detailed description of a Kentucky farmer named Arthur Shelby, who is about to lose his farm. Although he and his wife believe that they have a family-type relationship with their various enslaved African Americans, several of them are sold to raise the needed funds for the Shelbys to keep their farm. When one of the slaves overhears the Shelbys discussing plans to sell several others, one of them, Eliza, decides to run away with her son. This illustration by Jay Rial shows a fanciful depiction of Eliza fighting off two vicious dogs. (Courtesy of the Cincinnati Historical Society.)

Six

INDIVIDUALS AND CASES OF NOTE

FRANCES SCROGGINS-BROWN. Like many other African American Cincinnatians, Frances Scroggins-Brown was born in the South; in her case, in Virginia in 1819. Scroggins-Brown was a member of a small but emerging African American community in the Queen City that was involved in numerous Underground Railroad activities during the antebellum years. (Courtesy of the National Afro-American Museum and Cultural Center.)

JOHN M. LANGSTON. Langston was born free in 1829 in Louisa County, Virginia, as the youngest of four children. His father, Ralph Quarles, was a wealthy white planter and slaveholder, while his mother, Lucy Langston, was an emancipated slave of Indian and black ancestry. Both parents died in 1834 after brief, unrelated illnesses. Langston was left a sizable inheritance that ensured his financial independence. When he turned 14, young Langston enrolled in Oberlin College, where he became an outstanding debater. In 1849, he graduated from Oberlin, the fifth African American male to do so. Inspired by his early life in Cincinnati, Langston decided to get involved in the city's civil rights movement. As a result, at the invitation of Frederick Douglass, Langston was invited to deliver an impromptu speech to the National Black Convention in Cleveland, where he condemned those who refused to help fugitive enslaved African Americans. (From the Ohio Historical Society.)

WILLIAM WELLS BROWN. William Wells Brown was born in Lexington, Kentucky, in 1814, as the son of Elizabeth, a slave woman, and a white relative of his owner. After spending 20 years in slavery, William in 1834 developed a plan of escape. He spent the next two years working on a Lake Erie steamboat and running fugitive slaves into Canada. In the summer of 1834, he met and married Elizabeth Spooner, a free black woman. They had three daughters, one of whom died shortly after birth. Two years after his marriage, Brown moved to Buffalo, where he began his career in the abolitionist movement with the Western New York Anti-Slavery Society as an antislavery lecturer both in the United States and abroad. During his trips to Cuba and Haiti, Brown began to investigate to possibility of emigrating to one of those two islands. However, after several days of thinking, he decided to stay in the United States and continue with his abolition activities. (Courtesy of the Ohio Historical Society.)

JOHN P. PARKER. John Parker proclaimed, "I never thought of going uptown without a pistol in my pocket, a knife in my belt, and a blackjack handy. Day or night I dare not walk on the sidewalks for fear someone might leap out of a narrow alley at me." Born in 1827 in Virginia, Parker was a fearless conductor on the Underground Railroad. He was sold away from his mother at age eight and forced to walk on a line of chained slaves who traveled from Virginia to Alabama. After several unsuccessful escape attempts, he finally bought his freedom with the money he earned doing extra work as a skilled craftsman in 1845. Parker moved to Cincinnati and then to Ripley, where he became one of the most daring slave rescuers of the period. To those who followed him, Parker became primarily responsible for assisting runaways in crossing the Ohio to their freedom. Pictured here is the John Parker home. (Courtesy of the Ohio Historical Society.)

DAVID L. NICKENS, INITIAL PASTOR OF UNION BAPTIST CHURCH. The African Union Baptist Church, now known as the Union Baptist Church, was the first African American church in Cincinnati. On July 21, 1831, fourteen African American members of the Enon Baptist Church in Cincinnati decided to form their own congregation. This congregation, originally known as the African Union Baptist Church, was the second oldest African American congregation in the city. The reason they formed their own congregation was due to the discrimination, segregation, and racism present in the Enon Baptist Church. Whites at the Enon Baptist Church forced African American congregants to sit in the back even after they had regularly paid their tithes to the church. Initially, the African Union Baptist Church met in a member's home on Third Street between Plum and Elm Streets. In 1835, the congregation completed construction of a formal church building on Western Row, near Second Street. The following year, David Leroy Nickens, who was probably the first African American to be ordained as a minister in Ohio, became the church's pastor. (Courtesy of the National Underground Railroad Freedom Center.)

WILLIAM CASEY. Casey was a daring conductor on the Underground Railroad in Cincinnati. He was one of the few people who would row skiffs into Kentucky to help runaway slaves across the river. This image shows an example of the skiffs used on the river. (Courtesy of the Cincinnati Historical Society.)

THE UNKNOWN. Up and down the Ohio River, on both the Ohio and Kentucky side, numerous boats and skiffs were used to move different types of goods and products from one river city to another. On a number of occasions, African American fugitives used these types of water vehicles to escape to the North in pursuit of freedom. Pictured here is one such skiff. (Courtesy of the Ohio Historical Society.)

PETER FOSSET. Peter Fossett was born in 1815 at Thomas Jefferson's plantation, Monticello, in Virginia. Fossett's parents, Joseph and Edith Fossett, worked as Jefferson's blacksmith and head cook. According to Fossett, his childhood was relatively easy. After his second escape attempt, he was auctioned off by his owner. However, years later, with the assistance of some white Virginians, Joseph Fossett purchased his son, reuniting him with his family members in Cincinnati in 1850. (Courtesy of Dabney Publishing.)

SARAH FOSSETT. Sarah Fossett was born in 1826, in Charleston, South Carolina. Very little is known of her early life. However, by 1854 she had moved to Cincinnati, where she married Peter Fossett. The Fossetts became prominent members of Cincinnati's African American community and subsequently assisted hundreds of runaways via the Underground Railroad. (Courtesy of Dabney Publishing.)

WESLEYAN CEMETERY. Founded in 1843, Wesleyan Cemetery was the first integrated cemetery in Cincinnati. The grounds contain the remains of numerous prominent abolitionists, such as Zebulon Strong, John Van Zandt, and Rev. Henry Hathway of Covington, Kentucky. Also buried in the cemetery are about 600 Civil War veterans of various backgrounds, races, and ethnicities. (Courtesy of Richard Cooper.)

WESLEYAN CEMETERY AND THE UNDERGROUND RAILROAD. Along with being a significant cemetery for the remains of Civil War veterans as well as both prominent and little-known abolitionists, the grounds were also a very important stop on the Underground Railroad. It is rumored that several hundred fugitive African Americans used a safe house in the cemetery to hide for several days on their journey to freedom farther north. (Courtesy of Richard Cooper.)

SALMON P. CHASE. Born in 1808 in New Hampshire, Salmon P. Chase moved to Cincinnati, after he obtained his law degree from Dartmouth College and operated a private school for boys in Washington, DC, for a few years. Once in Cincinnati, many of Chase's legal activities focused on the elimination of slavery. He defended numerous fugitive African Americans against being recaptured and thus subsequently became known as the "attorney general for fugitive slaves." Chase also had an industrious career in American politics. From 1855 to 1860 he served as governor of Ohio and was twice elected to the US Senate. He resigned his senate seat to serve as President Lincoln's secretary of treasury during the Civil War. However, as a vocal critic of Lincoln's views on the issue of slavery and several military decisions, Chase attempted to resign his post in the administration three times before the president accepted his fourth offer in 1864. Chase is pictured at right and below, center. (Both, courtesy of the Cincinnati Historical Society.)

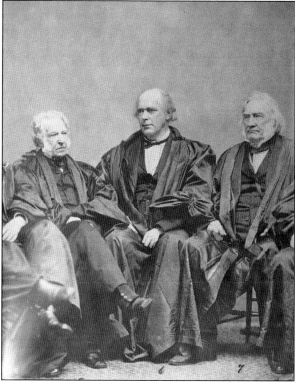

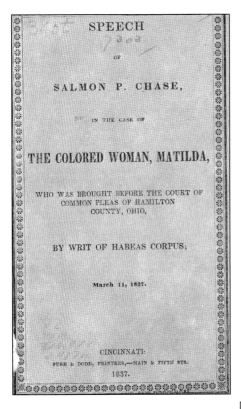

SPEECH

OF

SALMON P. CHASE,

IN THE CASE OF

THE COLORED WOMAN, MATILDA,

WHO WAS BROUGHT BEFORE THE COURT OF
COMMON PLEAS OF HAMILTON
COUNTY, OHIO,

BY WRIT OF HABEAS CORPUS;

March 11, 1837.

CINCINNATI:
PUGH & DODD, PRINTERS,—MAIN & FIFTH STS.
1837.

SPEECH OF SALMON P. CHASE. One of Chase's most famous cases was for a fugitive woman named Matilda in 1837. (Courtesy of the Cincinnati Historical Society.)

JOHN VAN ZANDT COURT CASE DOCUMENT. In 1842, John Van Zandt was accused and convicted of transporting a wagon of fugitive African Americans from Walnut Hills, Ohio, to Glendale, Ohio. In court, his defense attorney was Salmon P. Chase. However, Van Zandt died in 1847 before the case was tried. (Courtesy of the Cincinnati Historical Society.)

RECLAMATION OF FUGITIVES FROM SERVICE.

AN ARGUMENT

FOR THE DEFENDANT,

SUBMITTED TO

THE SUPREME COURT OF THE UNITED STATES,

AT THE DECEMBER TERM, 1846,

IN THE CASE OF

WHARTON JONES vs. JOHN VANZANDT.

BY S. P. CHASE.

CINCINNATI:
PRINTED BY R. P. DONOGH & CO., 168 MAIN STREET.
1847.

CINCINNATI COURTHOUSE. During the antebellum period, numerous highly contested civil rights cases were heard in the main courthouse in Cincinnati involving fugitive slaves as well as free blacks. Salmon P. Chase began his initial arguments in the Jones v. Van Zandt case, which eventually reached the US Supreme Court in 1847, at the local courthouse in Cincinnati during the early 1840s. (Both, courtesy of the Cincinnati Historical Society.)

HENRY BIBB. Known as "Walton" to his master, Henry Bibb was born enslaved in 1815 in Shelby County, Kentucky. As a youngster, many individuals told him that his father was a local white man named Henry Bibb, who happened to be a Kentucky state senator. However, young Henry never verified this rumor. In 1833, "Walton" Bibb married the biracial enslaved woman Malinda, who lived in Oldham County, Kentucky. They had a daughter named Mary Frances. Several years later in 1842, Bibb escaped from his owner's plantation in Kentucky and headed to Detroit, where he hoped save some money, build a home, and return to Kentucky to gain the freedom of his wife and daughter. After finding out that Malinda had been sold as a mistress to another white planter and moved to the deep South, Bibb began to focus on his career as an abolitionist. In 1850, he published his autobiography *Narrative of the Life and Adventures of Henry Bibb, An American Slave, Written by Himself,* which became one of the best known slave narratives of the antebellum era. (Courtesy of the Carolina Digital Library & Archives.)

BIRDS-EYE VIEW OF CINCINNATI.

JOHN FAIRFIELD. John Fairfield was the son of a Virginia slaveholding family, but he disagreed with his family practices and views on the topic of enslavement. As a young man, he became involved in many dangerous ploys to help runaways escape to freedom. One such episode included helping a childhood friend escape from Virginia to Ohio. However, upon his return to Virginia, Fairfield quickly learned that his uncle was planning to have him arrested. This situation only moved young Fairfield to become more involved in the abolition movement. Primarily using routes through Appalachia, he specialized in reuniting broken families. It is believed that Fairfield assisted some 28 enslaved persons living in Kentucky to cross the Ohio River near Lawrenceburg, Indiana. (Courtesy of the Cincinnati Historical Society.)

Rev. Calvin Fairbank. Fairbank, a Methodist minister, moved to Cincinnati in the 1840s. He operated a station on the Underground Railroad out of his home. In 1844, he was discovered trying to transport Kentuckian Lewis Hayden and his family. Reverend Fairbanks was sentenced to a 15-year prison term, of which he only served five years. (Courtesy of the Ohio Historical Society.)

Delia Webster. In Lexington, Kentucky, Delia Webster was a quite successful participant in Underground Railroad activities until she and Calvin Fairbank, in the fall of 1844, rented a carriage to take Lewis Hayden and his family to Maysville, and then across the Ohio River to Ripley, Ohio. Fairbank and Webster were caught, tried, and convicted. After serving a relatively short prison term, Webster went to Vermont and wrote a book about the ordeal. (Courtesy of the Library of Congress)

KENTUCKY JURISPRUDENCE.

A HISTORY OF THE TRIAL OF

MISS DELIA A. WEBSTER.

At Lexington, Kentucky, Dec'r 17-21, 1844,

BEFORE THE HON. RICHARD BUCKNER.

ON A CHARGE OF AIDING SLAVES TO ESCAPE FROM THAT COMMONWEALTH—WITH MISCELLANEOUS REMARKS, INCLUDING HER VIEWS ON AMERICAN SLAVERY.

WRITTEN BY HERSELF.

" HE THAT FILCHES FROM ME MY GOOD NAME,
ROBS ME OF THAT WHICH NOT ENRICHETH HIM,
AND MAKES ME POOR INDEED."—*Shakespear's Othello.*

VERGENNES:

E. W. BLAISDELL, PRINTER.

1845.

LEWIS HAYDEN. Lewis Hayden was one of Boston's most visible and militant African American abolitionists. He was born enslaved in Lexington, Kentucky, in 1812. His first wife, Esther Harvey, and a son, were sold to senator Henry Clay, who in turn sold them into the deep South. Hayden was never able to discover their whereabouts, so eventually he remarried a woman named Harriet Bell. Hayden and his new wife escaped with their son, Joseph, spending a few years in Cincinnati before moving to Canada in 1844, and then to Detroit in 1845. However, the Hayden family returned to Boston in 1846. There, Lewis ran a clothing store and quickly became a leader in the black community. In 1850, the family moved into a house at 66 Phillips Street and routinely cared for recently-escaped fugitives. (Courtesy of the Ohio Historical Society.)

LEWIS GARRARD CLARKE. Lewis Garrard Clarke was born in Madison County, Kentucky, seven miles from Richmond, in 1812. Depending on the source, Clarke's birth year is listed as 1812 or 1815. Clarke eventually obtained his freedom, became an abolitionist, and wrote his autobiography, titling it *Narrative of the Sufferings of Lewis Clarke*. In the beginning pages of this volume, Clarke discusses his years as a slave as well as his biracial family genealogy. Once the book was published in 1846, Clarke began to travel the United States telling his story. It was during one of these trips that he met Harriet Beecher Stowe, who was so impressed by Clarke that she based the character George Harris in *Uncle Tom's Cabin* on Clarke and his journeys. (Courtesy of Carolina Digital Library & Archives.)

WILLIAM P. NEWMAN. William P. Newman, who escaped from slavery in Virginia during the 1830s, became the pastor of the Union Baptist Church (now located on Seventh Street in downtown Cincinnati) and served in that position from 1848 to 1850. Before this, Newman studied for many years at Oberlin College and was a fiery orator. He traveled to Canada several times as an antislavery lecturer. Newman also was instrumental in the establishment of black schools in the Buckeye state and as an agent for the Ladies' Education Society of Ohio. However, when the Fugitive Slave Act of 1850 was enacted, Newman and his family moved to Ontario, Canada; he continued to fight for the freedom of African Americans, both enslaved and free persons of color, until he returned to Cincinnati in 1864. Two years later, in 1866, he died. (Courtesy of the National Underground Railroad Freedom Center.)

JOSIAH HENSON. Henson was born into slavery in Charles County, Maryland, in 1789. When he was a youngster, his father was punished for standing up to a slave owner, receiving 100 lashes and having his right ear nailed to the whipping-post, and then cut off. His father then was sold to a plantation owner in Alabama. Following his master's death, young Josiah was separated from his mother, brothers, and sisters when he was sold in an estate sale to a nearby owner. After his mother pleaded with her new owner, Isaac Riley, he agreed to buy back Henson so she could at least have her youngest child with her. Riley would not regret his decision, for Henson rose in his owner's esteem and was eventually entrusted as the supervisor of his master's farm, in Montgomery County, Maryland. However, in 1830, he escaped and moved to Ontario, Canada. While there, he founded a settlement and laborer's school for other fugitive slaves at Dawn, near Dresden, in Kent County. (Courtesy of the Ohio Historical Society.)

WALLACE SHELTON. Zion Baptist Church was organized in the fall of 1842 by Father Wallace Shelton with members from Union Baptist Church. The congregation was first located on Plum Street and, from this location, actively aided fugitive slaves through the Underground Railroad. The church became a prominent institution in the African American community of Cincinnati. (Courtesy of the Cincinnati Historical Society.)

WALLACE SHELTON GRAVE SITE, UNION BAPTIST CEMETERY. Union Baptist Cemetery, which contains the remains of Father Wallace Shelton and a number of African American Civil War veterans, is located in the Price Hill neighborhood of Cincinnati. Founded in 1884, the cemetery is the oldest Baptist African American cemetery in the city and was developed by members of the Union Baptist Church. (Courtesy of Richard Cooper.)

MARGARET GARNER. Enslaved with her four children on the Archibald Gaines farm in Boone County, Kentucky, Margaret and her husband, who was enslaved on a nearby farm, ran away one January night in 1856. Crossing the frozen Ohio River on foot, Margaret and her children went on to the home of an African American man in Cincinnati. But Gaines knew the location, and soon he and officers surrounded the house. Margaret saw that they cold not escape. Determined not to surrender her children to the horrors of enslavement, she took a knife and cut the throat of her young daughter and tried to do the same with her other children, but was stopped. The runaways were arrested and jailed. After a trial that lasted several weeks, the United States commissioner ruled that the runaways must be returned to the system of human bondage. Margaret was sold into the deep South. (Courtesy of the National Underground Railroad Freedom Center.)

CINCINNATI GAZETTE. Beginning in 1827, no other Cincinnati newspaper has ever reached the national stature of the *Cincinnati Gazette*. The *Gazette* (and its successors, the *Commercial Gazette* and the *Commercial Tribune*) was considered to be the finest newspaper published west of the Alleghenies during the antebellum period. The *Gazette* also regularly published controversial stories, such as the Garnet incident and subsequent case in 1850. (Courtesy of the Cincinnati Historical Society.)

JOHN JOLIFFE. Margaret Garner (called Peggy) was an enslaved African American woman before the Civil War who was both notorious and celebrated for killing her own daughter rather than allowing the child to be returned to slavery. Subsequently, Garner was taken to jail and tried for violating the Fugitive Slave Act of 1850. Her defense lawyer at the time was John Joliffe. (Courtesy of the Cincinnati Historical Society.)

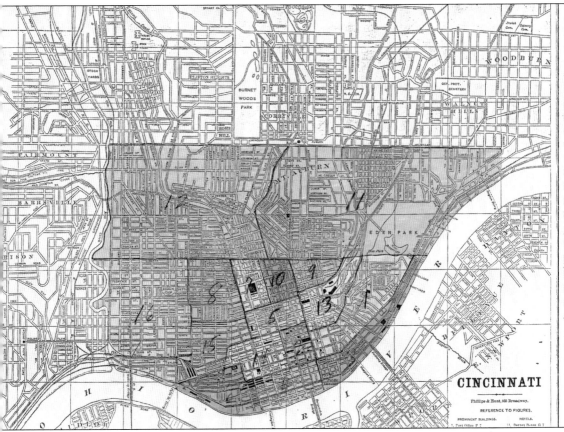

WARDS OF CINCINNATI, 1860. During the early 19th century, Cincinnati was an American boomtown in the heart of the country that rivaled the larger coastal cities in size and wealth. It was the first major city founded after the American Revolution as well as the first inland city. Germans were the first ethnic group that migrated to the city. However, several others came looking for employment and livable space. Despite the enactment of the state's "black laws," Cincinnati also became the destination for thousands of African Americans as well as a good number of both antislavery and proslavery men. Thus, on the eve of the American Civil War, part of the city's population wanted to support slavery while the other part actively assisted fugitives who sought freedom in the North. (Courtesy of the Cincinnati Historical Society.)

Seven

THE UNDERGROUND RAILROAD AND MEMORY

SPRING GROVE CEMETERY. During the 1830s and 1840s, Cincinnatians were demoralized by the recurrence of the cholera epidemic. Many of the city leaders expressed their concern over the lack of proper interment facilities. Resulting from this concern, members of the Cincinnati Horticultural Society formed a cemetery association in 1844. Salmon P. Chase and others prepared the articles of incorporation, lobbied with the state legislators, and persuaded them to grant a charter of corporation in 1845. (Courtesy of Richard Cooper.)

VIEW FROM SUPERINTENDENT'S RESIDENCE. Established as a non-profit cemetery in 1845, Spring Grove has served the community with dignity and respect for over seven generations and is a trusted part of the city's history. The view of the city itself from the grounds are breathtaking, especially from the superintendent's residence. (Courtesy of Cincinnati Historical Society.)

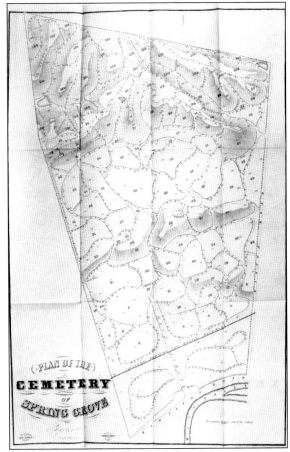

PLANNING LAYOUT MAP. Spring Grove Cemetery eventually allowed burials of African Americans and abolitionists. People active on the Underground Railroad are buried in the cemetery. (Courtesy of Cincinnati Historical Society.)

LEVI COFFIN BURIAL SITE. Buried in Spring Grove Cemetery along with thousands of other fallen heroes from the Civil War are a number of community activists, such as Catherine and Levi Coffin. It is said that the Coffins helped a little over 3,000 enslaved African Americans obtain their freedom in the North. Nevertheless, Spring Grove is not a typical cemetery because of its location and terrain. For instance, it took the group of founders years to find a location suitable for creating a picturesque park-like institution, a rural cemetery contiguous to the city yet remote enough not to be disturbed by expansion. The founders also sought to acquire enough land to be used for funerary purposes into the indefinite future, which could be embellished with shrubbery, flowers, trees, walks, and rural ornaments. At the consecration ceremony, the founders publicly proclaimed their hope that the natural setting would produce a contemplative atmosphere conducive to consolation, commemoration, and education. The first interment was made September 1, 1845. (Courtesy of Richard Cooper.)

Trail behind Spring Grove. The location, terrain, waterways, and wildlife at Spring Grove Cemetery provided a much needed burial facility that many Cincinnatians had wanted for decades. Over time, Spring Grove received much praise from various families and individuals. During the antebellum era, the region was populated with both proslavery and antislavery groups. The creek that runs behind Spring Grove provided perfect cover for enslaved African Americans to escape to freedom via the Underground Railroad by using the trails and paths that ran along the cemetery's outlying areas as well as along current-day Hamilton Avenue. (Courtesy of Richard Cooper.)

UNION BAPTIST CEMETERY. Union Baptist Cemetery is located at 4933 Cleves Warsaw Pike in Cincinnati. In 2002, it was listed in the National Register of Historic Places. This great honor occurred for a number of reasons, but especially because the cemetery is starkly different from many others on a variety of levels. (Courtesy of Richard Cooper.)

UNION BAPTIST CEMETERY. As the first African American cemetery in Cincinnati, this burial ground became the final resting place of a cadre of African American community leaders, military men, civil rights activists, and many members of the general population. For instance, almost one in 50 African American troops from the American Civil War are buried here. (Courtesy of Richard Cooper.)

WESLEYAN CEMETERY. Founded in 1843, Wesleyan Cemetery contains the remains of many of Cincinnati's most prominent abolitionists and antislavery activists, such as John Van Zandt. The grounds also contain the bodies of over 600 soldiers who fought in the Civil War. (Courtesy of Richard Cooper.)

WESLEYAN CEMETERY. Wesleyan Cemetery is a historic cemetery that was the first of its kind in Cincinnati, designed in a park-like fashion with winding drives, trees, and shrubs. Wesleyan Cemetery also was the first in the city to keep and maintain records of its burials and grounds, which it has done since its founding. The grounds are also known for their role in the Underground Railroad. (Courtesy of Richard Cooper.)

LEFT: The Moodys walk in front of their home.

MOODY RESIDENCE IN MOUNT HEALTHY. Mount Healthy was founded in 1817 as the village of Mount Pleasant. In 1850, the town renamed itself Mount Healthy following a massive and deadly cholera epidemic in the greater Cincinnati region, in which many citizens survived while those in the surrounding territory did not. The town was incorporated as a city in 1951. Decades before its incorporation, Mount Healthy was just a village that was a point more or less midway along the road that connected Cincinnati and Fort Hamilton. During the early 1800s, travelers who needed a place to stop, rest, and tend to their horses stopped in the village. Several homes in the town became stops on the Underground Railroad, where escaped slaves could seek shelter and aid on their flight northward to freedom. (Both, courtesy of the Cincinnati Historical Society.)

BUCKTOWN TODAY. During the antebellum years, Bucktown was one of two major African American communities in Cincinnati. Within these communities were a number of prominent and important African American churches, schools, businesses, and mutual aid societies. Today, this area is occupied by many Fortune 500 companies with headquarters in the Queen City. The importance of Bucktown cannot be underestimated in regards to its connection to the black community of Cincinnati during the antebellum years. Bucktown provided both free and enslaved African American Cincinnatians with a sense of dignity and power. (Both, courtesy of Richard Cooper.)

BLACK BRIGADE MONUMENT. The Black Brigade of Cincinnati was a military unit organized during the Civil War to protect the city from being attacked by the Confederates. The men who were part of the Black Brigade were among the first African Americans to be employed by the Union Army. Initially, Cincinnati did not allow African American males to join its volunteer militia. However, on September 2, 1862, many black Cincinnatians were rounded up by the local police and impressed into service to help construct emergency fortifications around the city. The labor was hard, and the police guards at times oppressed the workers by force. Later, Col. William M. Dickson took charge of the group and transformed them into the Black Brigade. In 2009, Cincinnati commissioned several sculptors, painters, and designers to create a Black Brigade Monument for a downtown park, which was dedicated several years later. (Both, courtesy of Richard Cooper.)

LYTLE PARK. Located in Cincinnati's central business district, Lytle Park features a floral display changing from tulips, magnolia, and crabapple in the spring, to annuals and perennials in the summer, and to annuals mixed with chrysanthemums in the fall. The 2.31-acre park, bounded by Fourth and Lawrence Streets, is the original site of the Lytle family homestead, built in 1809 by Gen. William Henry Lytle. The park also features an 11-foot-tall bronze statue of Abraham Lincoln. Lincoln came to the Queen City several times on the eve of the Civil War. (Both, courtesy of Richard Cooper.)

HOME OF SALLY AND SAMUEL WILSON. The home of Sally and Samuel Wilson was part of the emerging Underground Railroad movement in Cincinnati during the antebellum years. (Courtesy of Richard Cooper.)

ROBERT SCOTT DUNCANSON. Robert Scott Duncanson came to Cincinnati in 1840 as a free black man and taught himself to paint. He was the first African American artist to gain international fame, and his murals can be seen today at the Taft Museum. He traveled to Canada, Italy, Scotland, and England, where Queen Victoria bought one of his paintings.

THE NATIONAL UNDERGROUND RAILROAD FREEDOM CENTER. The National Underground Railroad Freedom Center opened in 2004. It is located on the banks of the Ohio River in downtown Cincinnati. The primary objective of the Freedom Center is to examine, discuss, and explore the story of the struggle for freedom in the United States through exhibits and programs that focus on America's battle to rid itself of the ugly scourge of slavery and treat all its citizens with respect and dignity. The focus of the museum is the compelling drama of the Underground Railroad. Although there was no actual railroad, there was a secret network of escape routes that existed in the years leading up to the Civil War. One major escape route passed through the region in and around Cincinnati. (Both, courtesy of Richard Cooper.)

BIBLIOGRAPHY

Bibb, Henry. *Narrative of the Life and Adventures of Henry Bibb: An American Slave*. New York: Negro University Press, 1969.

Bigham, Darrel E. *On Jordan's Banks: Emancipation and Its Aftermath in the Ohio River Valley*. Lexington, KY: The University Press of Kentucky, 2006.

Blight, David W. *Race and Reunion: The Civil War in American Memory*. Cambridge, MA: Harvard University Press, 2001.

Blight, David W., ed. *Passages to Freedom: The Underground Railroad in History and Memory*. New York: Smithsonian Books, 2004.

Franklin, John Hope and Loren Schweninger. *Runaway Slaves: Rebels and Plantation*. New York: Oxford University Press, 1999.

Gara, Larry. *The Liberty Line: The Legend of the Underground Railroad*. Lexington, KY: The University Press of Kentucky, 1961.

Griffler, Keith P. *Frontline of Freedom: African Americans and the Forging of the Underground Railroad in the Ohio Valley*. Lexington, KY: The University Press of Kentucky, 2004.

Hudson, J. Blaine. *Fugitive Slaves and the Underground Railroad in the Kentucky Borderland*. Jefferson, NC: McFarland & Company, 2002.

Siebert, Wilbur H. *The Underground Railroad from Slavery to Freedom*. New York: The MacMillian Company, 1898.

Sprague, Stuart S. *His Promised Land: The Autobiography of John P. Parker*. New York: W.W. Norton & Company, 1996.

Still, William. *The Underground Railroad*. Salem, MA: Ayer Company Publishers, 1968.

Taylor, Nikki M. *Frontiers of Freedom: Cincinnati's Black Community, 1802–1868*. Athens, OH: Ohio University Press, 2005.

Taylor, Nikki M. *America's First Black Socialist: The Radical Life of Peter H. Clark*. Lexington, KY: The University Press of Kentucky, 2013.

Trotter, Joe William Jr. *River Jordan: African American Urban Life in the Ohio Valley*. Lexington, KY: The University Press of Kentucky, 1998.

DISCOVER THOUSANDS OF LOCAL HISTORY BOOKS
FEATURING MILLIONS OF VINTAGE IMAGES

Arcadia Publishing, the leading local history publisher in the United States, is committed to making history accessible and meaningful through publishing books that celebrate and preserve the heritage of America's people and places.

Find more books like this at
www.arcadiapublishing.com

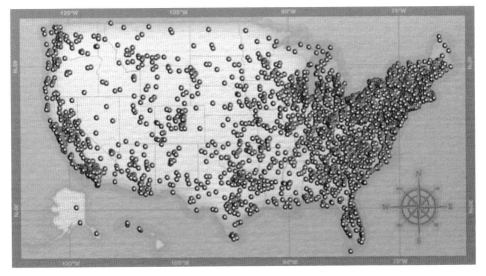

Search for your hometown history, your old stomping grounds, and even your favorite sports team.

Consistent with our mission to preserve history on a local level, this book was printed in South Carolina on American-made paper and manufactured entirely in the United States. Products carrying the accredited Forest Stewardship Council (FSC) label are printed on 100 percent FSC-certified paper.

MADE IN THE